7 Steps from Addiction to Sobriety

Written By Derrick Moore

This book is dedicated to my family and friends who all supported me through this journey. And of course, to all the men and women around the world actively struggling with addiction, and to those who are currently living in recovery. My heart goes out to you. I am on your team. And let me be the first to tell you:

#WeDoRecover
#RecoveryIsPossible

Hope you Enjoy.

Special Thanks:

To my mentor Michael Thompson for the guidance, and helping me start this vision, and to see it through. There is no way possible that this book would have happened without you. I appreciate all your contributions to this project. I appreciate you greatly brother.

Also to Corvaya Jeffries for all your help.

Table of Contents

Derrick Moore

Introduction

7 Steps From Addiction to Sobriety is a compilation of information, tools, tactics, methods, direction, and knowledge that I've compiled into a book which helped me unravel and untangle a 14-year span that lasted the duration of my entire adult life where I spent everyday as an alcoholic, a drug addict, or an inmate. That is not hyperbole; that is an actual fact. How about that for a statistic? I am not a licensed drug counselor or a treatment specialist; no. But I am an expert drug addict and a master mistake maker that did overcome his demons, correct his character to some degree, learn a new way to grow as a man, and achieve sobriety. This book is a step by step guide on how I did it.

Growing up in East Anchorage, Alaska, in a run down trailer and single mother home is not ideal. But none of it sapped any bit of my potential heading into the latter years of high school where I was placed in the prestigious advanced placement academic classes, was the top football player in the state, and had college athletic scholarship interest to match the talent. That's when the mistakes started to happen. At age 18, my senior year of high school; I got kicked off the basketball team for getting into a fight on the court, got expelled from school, lost my athletic future, became a felon, did my first bid of prison time, and became an alcoholic all in the same year. Every day of every year after that, I spent as an alcoholic, an inmate, or a drug addict struggling with addictions to heroin, meth, cocaine, crack, ecstasy, and alcohol. Until finally, two years into a 56 month federal prison sentence, still struggling with addiction while incarcerated, I came to the realization that something had to change. And something, at last, did start to change. This book is about that process.

Everything I've learned in my life, I learned the hard way; from losses, missed opportunities, to mistakes and bad decisions, to bad luck, heartbreak, and self-inflicted wounds. But in order to learn; something has to be doing the teaching. And nothing taught me more about life than my drug addiction. This book is about what I learned the hard way and how I overcame my setbacks and difficulties. This book is also about the *why* I know now that no struggle is permanent.

Chapter 1

Step 1: Any Positive Step In The Right Direction

Dealing with addiction, you'll come across many clichés. My least favorite cliche? "Once an addict always an addict." Another common saying is "one day at a time." Sound advice and a solid mantra but I like to use one that I think is better, and that is "one step at a time." Any positive step in the right direction? Yes, it's that simple. And there's three key components to the phrase:

- Any
- Positive
- Step in the right direction

I'll break down each component so you can get a better grasp of the quite vague and vast concept and by the end of the chapter you'll have a more clear picture of *why* you're taking only one step at a time. *What* it's going to do for you, *how* to do it, and *when* you're going to do it (but you already know the answer to that question. NOW). You're going to start now, but don't be intimidated. It's much easier than you think. Check this out.

Any

The definition of the adjective *"any"* in the Merriam-Webster dictionary is as follows: (a) one or some indiscriminate type or kind (b) one or another taken at random (c) used to indicate one selected without restriction. That's the Webster definition and that's the definition that I mean when I say ANY positive step. And the fun part is, you get to choose. It's all up to you. And I don't say that to apply any pressure whatsoever. This isn't about seeing the motivational quotes online about "getting off your ass right now and doing it." It's not about the gurus of inspiration and wisdom telling you, "this is how you do it and this is the only way," no. It's about you relying on yourself. There isn't only *one* way to find *a* way out of any struggle, including addiction. This is about you finding *your* way, which is always the *best* way.

You know better than anyone else what you're capable of doing, what you want to do, what you have time to do, what you would be willing to do (and most importantly), what you'd be willing to *keep* doing. That's where you're going to start. Figuring out what exact step you'd like to take, out of the millions of options, to start improving your life. That's it. We're starting small. Starting simple. But we're starting. As soon as we figure out: by doing what, and how.

Maybe you actually enjoy reading. Well you can learn a lot from reading so that's an option. The self-help genre, in regards to literature, has been one of the fastest growing categories as far as reading material is concerned and for good reason. Reading, one of the oldest, tried and true methods of learning, could be a perfect place to start.

Maybe you, at some point in your life, were dedicated to fitness and have been thinking about getting back in the gym, but don't know where to start or what workouts to do, or think you don't have time. That's fine; Google it. Do a little research. Find a basic workout schedule and routine and start there. Start small and with short time periods. Fitness is a big part of my sobriety today, but when I started, I started with the most basic by all measure, novice routines for 20-minutes a day. You don't have to do a lot, just do some.

Maybe it's something you'd like to try that's new like writing down or repeating affirmations, journaling, yoga, or reading the Bible. Or maybe there's a character flaw that's been hindering you a lot of your life you'd like to improve upon like depression, sadness, guilt, shame, or pessimism.

Find a book or a podcast based on improvement in those areas and start learning about it for 30-minutes a day. It can even be as simple as 20-minute nature walks or listening to daily informal podcasts or YouTube channels geared around personal growth and wellness. Just *something*. That's all we're looking for at this stage of this process. Something, anything, to infuse into our daily life(which if you're struggling with addiction), I'm sure revolves around much of the same, and not much of it good. Virtually you have unlimited options to choose from. And if you're still confused, you have the greatest resource in your hand known to man: Your smart phone.

We get caught up on the tail end of our smartphones; the social media, the scrolling. So much so, that we actually under utilize it. We can run a business, correspondence across the globe, and we can research ways to improve our lives. Yes. You're going to Google "best ways to improve your life," or "best ways to start to change your life," or something towards the tune of which kind of step you're contemplating taking. We all know how to Google something to find something out. And what's going to pop up? Millions of results and millions of answers. Approach the suggestions with an open mind, find one that suits you, that makes sense to you, and roll with it.

I can hear the skepticism already, *"what are these random people on Google/YouTube going to tell me? What do they know about addiction? How can Google help me fix my life?"* It's not so much Google, YouTube, or the internet that's doing it. It's a research tool used to steer you in the right direction, and a very powerful one at that.

Trust me I've been there. With the incredulousness, the pessimism, and the skepticism. But the entire process of change stops and starts with your inability or ability to be open minded. To initiate any type of change, even at its inception, you must have some inkling of belief that one of these practices, one of these methods, one of these books, one of these exercises, one of these search results, that this *one step,* can actually help you. You have to actually believe that it can do you good. And that's coming from a naturally born pessimist. I know now, firsthand, that this is what hindered any ignition of progress during my 14-year span of prison and addiction.

I never thought self-help books would teach me anything. I never believed meditation would calm my mind. I never thought journaling would help. So I simply never tried. So I never took any step, never moved in the right direction, and as my addictions would get worse, I would start taking steps in the wrong direction. And my life would get worse right along with it. But when you actually think about it, one of these books, meditations, exercises, diets, these random search results, actually *helping you?* In layman's terms it's actually not that far fetched, and kind of asinine to believe anything other than that they *could* help you.

This article, this book, this podcast, this diet, this workout; generated from this random search result, or random podcast, from this random person, learned it from another random person, who learned from another person, and now you're the millionth random person that's about to learn it. Most of what we learn is passed down from generation to generation, and has helped millions of people. On top of that, if you think that it will help, IT WILL.

I know when I had to pick my "*any*," out of the many options, I had no phone and limited resources. But I had to figure something out to change the way I had been living my life the entirety of my adulthood. I had very few options to choose from as far as avenues to pursue in order to change my life. That's because, well. When I started to actually change my life; I was in federal prison.

———————

In prison, when I decided to make my change, it actually wasn't a decision to change my entire life. Just a decision to take a step to change a *part* of my life. I was about a year and a half away from being released from a 56-month federal prison sentence for a federal crime I committed two days after being released from a heroin detox facility. My heroin and meth addictions broke me down to the lowest form of human I have ever experienced. Hopeless, helpless, broke, broken, and suicidal. Now sitting in prison because of a crime I committed to feed my addiction, I had gone straight from the streets to prison, and was able to maintain my drug habit while incarcerated; a sentence I was supposed to be using solely for the purpose of soul-searching, rectifying my life, and reforming my character.

You could actually argue that I was getting worse. I had made no progress, made no attempt to progress, or made no attempt to change my life or my character. And I lived every single day in fear of jeopardizing my freedom by two to eight months by being caught using an illegal substance in prison after failing a urine analysis test. Literally risking my freedom, jeopardizing being back in my family's lives, still addicted, and didn't even attempt to get clean. Negative. Negative. Negative. Negative.

So in the middle of my new addiction, with my freedom *hopefully* looming in the near future, I had to do something. The truth is, in the back of my mind the entire time, *I knew* I had to do something. I just didn't know where to start. So I never did. In prison, your resources are limited. But you do have advantages; structure, less distractions, plenty of time. But none of that means anything if you don't do *something*. Do *anything*. And that first "*anything*" I decided to do, was to learn. Specifically read. More specifically reading self-help books. That's where I started to take my steps in the right direction.

When I chose to pick up that first book to take that first step, I was still getting high in prison. Meth, heroin, suboxone, k-2 spice, whatever drug I could get my hands on. Selling my belongings, my commissary, hustling, and gambling to feed my addiction. Nearly identical to my conduct I displayed when I was free trying to feed my addiction. And not for one second did it cross my mind that this book would help me get sober, stay clean, or not be an addict. Never did I even think I wouldn't continue to get high today, tomorrow, or when I got out. Staying clean wasn't even a goal.

What actually prompted me to take a step to change was a snarky comment by my old cellmate who was the consummate optimism. He got tired of my constant pessimism and negativity and shouted at me one day, "bro, I'm tired of your negative energy. I don't want to deal with all your negative bullshit right now!" It took me back a little. I thought to myself, *'I don't want to be THAT guy. That guy everyone thinks is negative, giving off the bad vibe.'*

One sentence, one altercation, prompted me to look at a character flaw: my pessimism. That's what I wanted to change. I wanted to become more optimistic. It had nothing to do with addiction or sobriety. But an adjacent character flaw was what I initially sought out to fix. It didn't matter that it had nothing to do with addiction. It was a step in the right direction and that's all you need.

So how do you work on becoming more optimistic? What book can teach me how to think more positively? Well, how about a book written by Norman Vince Peale called **Power of Positive Thinking?** Duh. My first self-help book I've ever read. A book where I fully half-assed. Skipped pages, read about 30 pages out of 100 something. But in those 30 pages, a sentence here, a sentence there, practice I tried, information I took; I learned some. And wouldn't you know it? It had an effect. What I learned did help me feel a little more optimistic. That *little more* was a little more than I had before I read those 30 pages.

After that little bit of progress, a book called ***Unf*ck Yourself(1)*** written by Gary John Bishop crossed my path. For one, I loved the title. I felt like I've been fucking myself all my life and I would very much like to *"unfuck"* myself. And on the back of the book it asked *"Stuck in a rut?"* Yes. *"Cynical?"* Yes. *"Bored?"* Yes. Yes x3. So I opened the book. I read a sentence here, a chapter here, took some notes there, highlighted this, highlighted that, remembered this. The book resonated for me. I *learned* from it. Learning. That's what prompted me to read this second self-help book. But I needed to read that first book to even know that learning was possible from these books. Without the results from that first step, I would have never taken the time to read the second, or the third.

You're A Bad Ass by Jen Sincero was the third book I read. A book I had to fully activate my open mindedness to even open the book. The cute cover, the bubbly title, the female writer. I thought, *'what the fuck is this lady going to teach a gangster, three-time felon, and heroin addict about how to fix his life?'* But I gave it a shot anyway and I learned again. I learned how to be more optimistic and how to raise my frequency. Never even heard about this *"energy"* called frequency before in my life. But she taught me about it. I learned about kindness and self-love. Concepts before that were all foreign to me. But learning about them allowed me to grow.

Not a single word about drug addiction. Not a single thought crossed my mind about sobriety. But I chose. I chose to make a step. That *"any"* choice for me was reading. But it can be *anything* for you. It's a simple decision to start building on something and building on a positive foundation and that's all the step requires. Is that you're choosing to learn and to start stepping in a different direction. In this case, that direction is a positive one. That's the next part. It can't just be any step. It HAS to be a positive one.

Positive

I believe in intuition. I believe in gut feeling. I do believe that every human has this voice in the back of your mind that contains the wisdom and the prudence to decipher the difference between right and wrong, good or bad, positive and negative. I believed I always possessed that same quality. And that's where the drugs came into play. I used the aid of narcotics to blind my vision and blur the line that separated right and wrong. To effectively eliminate contrition and fear of consequences. And during my addiction, I had no fear of consequences, retribution, or repercussions for my actions. In regards to punishment I might receive as far as incarceration, how it impacted my family, or how it would negatively affect my character—while I was high—I didn't care one bit about any of that.

Before prison, when I decided to (at the lowest point in my life struggling to maintain my heroin addiction and meth addiction, withdrawing three to five days out of the week for months) finally take a step, I had a plan. A two-part plan. First, I needed to get clean. Second, I needed money. Okay, that doesn't sound like a bad plan right? Getting clean and having money. We can all agree that on a fundamental level, that sounds like a good plan.

So I needed to get clean and I needed some money. Bet. That's the plan. For an addict, the overall outlook for that plan seems to be a move in the right direction. As an addict, in my addicted mind, accomplishing those two things, you could not have convinced me that accomplishing those two goals would not have been a move in the right direction. And in reality, that's exactly how I felt. But my steps. The steps I chose to achieve those two goals, were negative steps. Not positive steps.

I was focused on the direction that lied in the future instead of the quality of steps that I chose to get there, but I wasn't aware of that. I was convinced that by obtaining money, and getting to sobriety, my life would be instantly fixed. I was *sure* that this was how to rectify my life. That if I took steps in *that* direction, no matter what the quality of the steps were, my life would definitely get better. And I did take those steps in that direction. But they were negative steps. And my life didn't get better. It got much worse.

I wanted the quickest, fastest, least resistive path of sobriety. So I chose to go to a seven day detox; one I knew I could sneak Suboxone and Xanax into so I wouldn't have to endure the fullness of the detox. I would get out after seven days, get a vivitrol shot (a 30-day opiate blocker), which would make me "*clean*" off heroin. But I could still get high on meth and would continue to use meth. **Right direction**: get clean off opiates. **Negative steps to get there**: use Xanax for the detox and continue to use meth to feed my urge to get high.

Part two. Now I needed the money. I needed another shortcut. So 48-hours after I was released from that detox facility, high on meth, I executed step two of my plan where I stooped to the lowest form of morality I was capable of, committing my most shameful act and egregious crime; and I robbed a bank. **Right direction:** get financially secure. **Negative step to get there:** commit a federal crime.

I was convinced that if I got clean and I got the money in my pocket, I would be headed in the right direction. And I did that. I actually did it. I actually executed a plan I believed in. It took every bit of discipline I had to get through that detox and get that shot. But I did it. It took every bit of courage I could muster up to rob a bank. But I did it. And there wasn't an ounce of doubt in my mind that *this* plan, was *the* plan, that was going to finally get my life back on track. I didn't think for one second it would fail. But in reality it had no chance to succeed. There wasn't a single second after the detox and after the robbery that I felt like my life had improved one bit. That's because there is no reality in where you will harvest positive fruit from negative seed. No matter how you feel in your mind. No matter what the drugs were convincing me of. If it's wrong, its not going to get you right.

I took negative steps to get where I *thought* I needed to go, so I was actually, the entire time, heading in the wrong direction. I changed nothing about myself and nothing about who I was around; none of my conduct or thoughts. I was essentially an addict with the same bad habits and character flaws with money in my pocket and increasing enclosure of depression, and a newfound, overwhelming, longing to commit suicide. My life had gotten much worse after the steps I took.

We all have goals and objectives we want to complete; results we want to realize. That's why we take the steps. And it's no different with addiction. But I think we can all agree that there is a right way and there is a wrong way of going about it. If your choice of your *"any"* step to take is to read because you like reading, don't pick up the **Lord of the Rings** trilogy because you won't gain anything. It's not a negative step but this is about improvement, so pick up a self-help book if reading is your choice.

Maybe you'd like to learn through YouTube. Well, don't just scroll all day watching funny, viral videos. Find a positive informal program or channel to watch on You-Tube that's going to help you grow as a person. It's about finding that no gray area, not up for discussion, positive step. We know if you meditate, you'll be more calm. If you exercise you'll be more fit and healthy. If you pray you'll have more faith. These are the types of positive steps that we're trying to formulate into habit to get you progressing and moving in the right direction. That's the next part and if you've got the first two parts down, the third is a piece of cake. There's no way to screw it up. You'll be guaranteed to be stepping in the right direction.

Step in the right direction

To step means to progress. It means we are moving forward. And if your choice of the *"any one"* is a *"positive one,"* it is a certainty; not a hopefully or a mere possibility. It is a guarantee that your steps will be in the right direction. That's based off of a simple universal law that is easy to understand without means of any extensive details. And that is: 'Cause and Effect.' Or 'You Reap what you Sow.' Both one in the same. The perfect, live example of this (albeit the opposite form), is a drug habit.

During my drug addiction with every relapse, the longer I was strung out, the worse my life became. The more I used, the more I needed to use. And the more I used, the worse my life became. The more I stole, the more I lied, the more crimes I committed, the more depressed I became, the less happiness I experienced, and the more peace evacuated my soul. The more negative seeds I sowed, the more negative results I reaped. And my character and my circumstances followed suit in lockstep which is how it will always work.

You cannot alter the law of cause and effect. You cannot get good fruit from bad seeds. But the opposite is also just as much 100% a fact, you cannot get bad fruit from good seeds. That is universal law. It cannot be altered.

But that's a good thing. Because that's how we're going to use it to our advantage. With every page of a self-help book you read, with every minute of that law of attraction podcast you listen to, every push-up you do, with every affirmation you write down or repeat, or whatever step you choose, you are actively planting good seeds. Positive seeds, that will later undeniably sprout good fruit.

This is *"step one"* and it's a positive step in the right direction. Which means you are active in the process of progressing no matter what your circumstances look like, no matter where your addiction has your life. With participating in even the most minimal form of something positive, for a short amount of time, even if you don't feel like you're progressing, you are. Even if you're still getting the negative *"minus 1's,"* you can still add positive gains. Just like I was when I was beginning my transformation. I was still getting high, still lazy, still negative. But my mind, body, and soul was already used to the negative *"minus 1's."* It wasn't used to the positive *"plus 1's."* That's why those 30 pages of that first self-help book I half-assed my way through actually had a profound effect. The positive gains, the steps in the right direction, were a shock to my spirit. That's what ultimately stunted my regression and was the ignition of my progression. I started unraveling 14 years of prison, alcoholism, and a drug addiction with a 30-minute a day self-help book reading habit.

Addiction can be gloomy, daunting, dreary, and discouraging. That's because it revolves and feeds off negativity. Your circumstances are negative, people around you are negative, your thoughts are negative, your actions are negative. In this step you are subtly infusing positivity back into your life and out into the universe. That 30-minutes, that hour, that 20-minutes, whatever you choose, be as flexible as you need to be. No matter where you are in your addiction, you are getting positive gains that will better prepare you for when the opportunity to reach sobriety presents itself. You're preparing yourself, right now, for that day to come. Because it's going to come.

There are no special requirements to taking any one step in the right direction. No over-the-top, willpower, no ultimatum, no enhancement of capabilities. The only requisites are adequate effort and consistency. It will not work without either of those two things. I know addiction can drain your effort. It's a tiresome burden. That's why we're starting small. Consistency can also be difficult because an addiction makes discipline such a weak spot. But that's why we're starting with small time periods. 20 to 30 minutes, up to an hour a day. You have to find a way no matter what you're going through (high, withdrawing, clean, urging, etc.) to find the time for a small increment of time to implement and take your step. That's as hard as this step will get. Effort and consistency.

We have enough bad habits as it is. Right now, we're searching for one good habit. Just one. And we're going to start building one good habit. Then we'll start building a foundation on top of that one good habit once it is built to ensure that we get our positive step in the right direction everyday, no matter what. And with those steps upward, soon you'll be putting some distance between who you were, and who you're becoming.

————————

I know for me, climbing out of addiction felt like climbing a mountain. I had dug myself such a deep hole that I would look up at the top of the mountain and look at the many steps I needed to climb and it was daunting. I would be discouraged and intimidated and I would simply not try. Thinking "*I took me a million steps back and it'll take me a million steps to get back where I started and it's gonna take me a million years to do it.*" But when I had my head tilted up, looking up staring disheartened at this Goliath of a mountain I had to climb; I missed the entire point. And that was, *'what I could do where my feet were planted at this very moment.'* I didn't have to be capable of climbing one million steps at once. In fact, it's not possible. No one is capable of taking one million steps at once. It's not something you can do. There is no million step, *step*.

All I ever had to be capable of doing was taking *one* step. Every millionth step started with one. And there's not any one step that any one person is not capable of taking and making. We can all take one step. We are all capable of that. Trying to take too many steps at once is where many people get overwhelmed, frustrated, and ultimately give up on their resolutions. You need that solid first step, because you *need* what you learn, what you *gain* in that first step, to be more *capable* of making the second step. What you learn in the second step is what makes you capable of taking the third step.

It's about getting those positive gains, those *"plus 1's."* Every positive gain, every plus one is like a vote going in the ballot box for the person you want to become. And we all know the person with the most votes wins. Keep putting votes in that box. Now you still might be getting the negative 1's, but don't be discouraged. I was sitting in prison, with a jailhouse addiction, 30 pounds overweight when I read that first self-help book. But I learned. That little bit of knowledge gained (my positive result), was what compelled me to read the second one. Which was my second step. And that's when you'll start to learn about the actual power of positivity.

Your positive steps in the right direction will always outweigh your negative steps in the wrong direction. That's because positive energy moves twofold. It's not only in addition to your progression, but it's also a subtraction from your regression. A fancy way of saying, *"you're going to find your way out of your troubles much faster than the time it took you to get yourself in them."* And that's how we start beating your addiction, by taking *"any positive step in the right direction."*

Hardaway Learning Suggestion:

1. Identify a character flaw or personality trait you would like to change about yourself i.e. pessimism, bad attitude, low-self esteem, depression, etc.

2. Use Google to search "Best books to help with (insert character flaw)"

3. Buy the book, read the book for 30-minutes a day, take notes in a journal, practice any suggestions the book might give as advice on how to cope with said character flaw.

4. Be consistent with the habit.

Chapter 2

Step 2: Open Your Mind To A Power Outside of Yourself

Now that we have taken positive steps in the right direction, we finally have a little breathing room. We began the process of progress by mustering up some of our own latent inner strength to help ourselves. That's the first step. That's a start. But now, we're seeking further help. By a *"power outside of ourselves."* This whole process of change will be a whole lot easier if you're open minded to the options that are available out there, to aid, and assist you on your journey to change. But there's a key component to this phrase *"power outside of yourself,"* which is a very broad statement that could mean a lot of things. And in this case, in this step, it can, and does mean a lot of things. And it is intended to be that way.

So what does *"a power outside of yourself"* mean? Well, it can mean a lot of things; God, Goddess, The Universe, Source Energy, a Higher Power, spirituality. But I left it out of the step description because it's absolutely imperative that which ever one of these powers outside of yourself you choose to follow and learn about, is one that you feel comfortable with learning about. That you feel comfortable with taking steps towards getting connected with. One that aligns with your personal beliefs and you will be open minded to receiving the intended support and guidance that these powers are universally known for.

So every one of these options for a *"power outside of yourself"* are on the table. Even ones I did not mention. Ones that you might know about, that I do not. As regards to the simplification of this chapter, I will refer to this power as Spirituality, or as a Higher Power. And if you already have a preferred spirituality, even better. You already know which way to go you. You already have some base foundational knowledge about spirituality. That's a perfect place to start for this step. Your ahead of the curve. But if you don't, the choice will be yours to decide which direction to take. It is in no way a disadvantage to have a complete clean slate to learn about new things. In some-ways its an advantage. Either way is perfectly fine.

Whether you have an established foundation of spirituality that you believe in already, or you're starting at an open minded starting point; to *start* believing is the step. Regardless of where you're starting from. The actual belief itself is what is going to bring us closer to receiving those abundant benefits from one of the most ancient, largest, tried and true sources of self-help ever known to mankind. A divine source of self-development that helps millions, daily, grow and overcome. And that divine source *is* spirituality.

Spirituality, or believing in a Higher Power greater than ourselves, offers a myriad of benefits. Connecting to this belief can bring you: guidance, contentedness, confidence, support; that are all essential in the raising of virtues like: hope, faith, and optimism. Virtues that are based on believing in something that you cannot see. But the essence of spirituality is to form a foundation upon which these virtues can be built upon. And that is going to be our step. To use spirituality to our advantage, in the middle of our current struggles, to eradicate our lower base characteristics, like pessimism, fear, and doubt. And to learn a way to morph, and transform, and adjust those characteristics that come along with addiction, to some of the higher frequency traits known to man, like: optimism, hope, and faith.

This is not intended to steer you to any specific religion, church, or set of beliefs, because the choice is solely up to you based on what your needs are, and what ideas you'll be open to being receptive to. But all these theologies; God, Buddhism, the Universe, Law of Attraction, Higher Power, Source Energy; are available. Maybe its a combination of a few, or one specific. Its all up to you. I'm comfortable with two separate ideals, that form my belief. A Higher Power; I believe in God. And I believe in *"Energy."* An energetic source of energy that formulates, what I, and some call *"the Universe."*

I did not grow up in a religious household with any religion, or even go to church consistently. Did I grow up believing in God? Sure. I think I did. My spirituality, this vital part of my sobriety, I learned about, on my own, from scratch because I never actually took the time to learn about God. To develop a belief, and comprehend what it meant to actually *have* faith. And my understanding of the Universe came way later in life in my early 30s, sitting, searching desperately for something to flip the switch, to break that chain of years of prison and addiction I had endured since I was 18 years old. And I'll tell you, when that light actually flipped for me, and what I consider to be the foundation that my spirituality has been built upon, my life was honestly changed. Not immediately. But it changed. The change need time to take root. But I needed *a* change. That's what I needed. And *when* that light flipped for me; was actually during my federal sentencing for a bank robbery.

———————

I mentioned vicious cycles of addiction and prison, starting at the age of 18. At 18 I went to jail for the first time, got kicked off the basketball team, lost my college athletic opportunities, got expelled from school, and was convicted for my first felony: a robbery of six dollars on March 14, 2008(Yes, you heard me correct; a robbery of 6 *dollars*). A crime that I did not commit, but was involved in, and ultimately changed the entire course of my life. There would be no college sports, no clean record, and no more innocence. A felon for the rest of my life, I turned to the streets, and my life began spiral out control steadily for the next 14 years.

Fast forward to April 2, 2018, the day the bank robbery was committed and you'll see a significant discrepancy. Not the difference between the six dollars and the bank heist; but the actual *dates* the crimes took place. Federal sentencing guidelines are based off *"points"*. Points are based off your criminal history. Violent crimes, like robberies, give you more points, and two of the same violent crime can make you a career criminal. Which could be an extra 6 points. Which ends up equating to nearly a 6-8 year increase. The more points you have, the more time you do.

But those dates I talked about; March 14, 2008 and April 2, 2018? Those dates are 10 years and 18 days apart. Any crime after 10 years is expunged from your record and from being calculated to your federal sentencing point total. Not only dropping my tabulated point total by subtracting a violent crime and a felony off of my record, but excluding me from possibly being charged with a career criminal enhancement. Effectively dropping me from looking at 12 to 16 years to 4 to 6 years. Complete and utter luck. The only good luck I've had in over a decade.

I remember my mentality while I was addicted to heroin, depressed, and suicidal. There was no strategy to avoid any steep penalty. I didn't even care about my life at all. I did not plan the alignment of the dates, I knew nothing about the potential of spending a decade plus in prison. Nor did I even care enough about my life to even consider trying to avoid it. But when I got that good news, a simple thought crossed my mind, a common phrase, a social media hashtag, a cliche left my lips, and entered my mind *"I got blessed"*. And I actually meant it. *Is that blessing?* Absolutely. *Who's doing the blessing?*

I just remember the magnitude of that moment. The thoughts that crossed my mind. Much different from the thoughts that had crossed my mind the last 14 years, the last year, the last month, the last day, the last minute before I got the news. *Did I deserve a blessing?* No I did not. I put myself in no position. I put no effort in, had no strategy, the blessing was in no way shape or form my doing. So what was it? That's the first time I contemplated that maybe; God, spirituality, the Universe, a power greater than myself, was real. That maybe *this* is my second chance.

There is a real version of myself that would have gotten that same good news, and laughed, and thought *'haha you thought you were going to give me 10 years, but your only gonna give me 5, I WIN.'* And instantly made plans to get back to the same exact behavior that got me locked up once I was released. But at that moment, who I was at that *one* moment then, decided to take that good break, that good luck, and look at that same situation from a different perspective. *'That maybe there is such a thing as Gods Plan'*. *'That maybe this is my second chance'*. I viewed that good break from a different vantage point, that planted the first seed of hope I've had in over a decade. And that seed was rooted in Spirituality.

Although, I would continue on with my destructive behavior well into the 56 month federal prison sentence I ended up receiving; picking up in jail house drug addiction and overeating addiction to accompany it around a year and a half away from my release. Still addicted, still lazy, still negative. Truth is, that seed of spirituality I had spoke of in the previous paragraph, hadn't affected me. Not my conduct, my thoughts, my mentality, or my circumstances whatsoever. Not even my addiction for that matter. But I always kept that good break that affected my future so profoundly, in the back of my mind. Always knowing that *this was* my second chance. That I *had* to figure something out to change my ways. Even though I wasn't acting like it.

But when COVID-19 hit society, and the prison system, it caused a continual 23-hour lockdowns for days and months at a time. Forcing me to take the time to do some soul-searching, reading, learning and working out. Time I needed to take to do those things, but did not ask for. I got another break in the form of a coincidental circumstance with the mandatory lockdown, and by no doing of my own. But the time to sit by myself, in a 8x12 room, with nowhere to go, nowhere to hide, and no drugs to get high on, was necessary. I needed it, but there was no way for me to make that happen on my own. And if I could make it happen on my own, there is no telling if I would have seized the opportunity. I would like to think that I would. But we'll never know. A Higher Power could have only orchestrate that size of a shift in one's life. Line up the dominoes *that* perfect, put me in *that* ideal of a situation, at the right time, and the right place, all at once. That's what I believe. I actually was able to view these occurrences as a sign from above that *this* was my time, my chance, to save my life. It was that change in perspective, that motivated me to seize the opportunity I was presented with. And in that cell, during that covid lockdown, that's where I started to read my first pages of those books I mentioned in the previous chapter. And that's where my transformation begin.

Were these occurrences(the sentencing, the lockdown), luck? Sure they were. But did they help me? Absolutely. What could your life look like if your luck changed? If these circumstances that you did not ask to be placed upon yourself, were working for you, and not against? During a 23 hour lockdown, for a couple months straight I began reading, writing, learning, meditating, working out; within months I started feeling like a completely new man. I could *feel* the change. Clear from the withdraw-als, 20 pounds lighter, enlightened with knowledge from numerous self help books that I've read over that period. I was filled with positivity, hope, expectancy, for the first time in over a decade and a half. I felt *different*. I could *feel* the difference.

———————

My spirituality would take full form out of the blue, by a series of unforeseen events, that I believe was a touch of God. One day, minding my business, the Unit Coun-selor knocked on my door and told me to "pack my bags". '*Pack my bags?*." She said, "pack your bags." Because '*I was going home*'. '*WTF?!*' .I couldn't understand it. I had put in no appeals, applied for no compassionate release, and still had about 8 months to serve on my sentence. This was completely out of the blue. Out of nowhere, I couldn't believe. Understandably, to an inmate, or someone who has served time before, there is no greater feeling than realizing that you have finally approached that day when you're finally about to gain back your freedom. No birth-day, no holiday, no gift can compare.

The biggest blessing I could have imagined, fell right into my lap, out off thin air. Come to find out; the Alaskan halfway house was in desperate need for Alaskan inmates to feel their empty beds in order not to lose their contract with the feds. And luckily for me, and a friend of mine named '*Church*' (also from Alaska), got the call. I went from 240 days to 24 for days left to serve in 20 seconds. My luck had officially changed.

Getting to the quarantine cell with Church. A holding cell you must be placed in in order to be released, we spent the first hour thinking '*How in the hell did this twist of fate happen? Was it real? Man, his law of attraction thing really works. This positive energy thing really works.*' I had spent so much time rewiring my brain, my thoughts, my conduct, my mood, reforming my character, and now I actually had real proof that you can change your ways, and your circumstances will change right along with them. It was a great moment.

The more I wrapped my head around this significant blessing, I started to feel this presence. This physical energy penetrate my being. That elated feeling I felt, that big smile, that boost in my spirit, I was convinced was a presence of God. I could feel it. Nothing like that has ever happened in my entire life. An actual feeling caused by an experience that convinced me that *He* was real. But *this* experience convinced me God was real. Even after what happened next.

41

As much as the moment brought in the feelings of bliss from the feeling of God actually blessing my life, I actually learned a different lesson that is another cornerstone of my spirituality. And that is: Faith vs fear. As much delight as that moment brought. As significant as the realization that God was actually real brought to my life. There was still this little bit of doubt and fear that it was all good to be true. And sure enough.

About 5 days after receiving a new release date, about 20 days from being brought back home, walking back from the shower, the counselor looked me straight in the eyes and said "I gotta talk to you". And I knew exactly what time it was. I knew exactly what she was going to tell me. She said, "We made a mistake, you won't be getting released". I was heartbroken and angry. A familiar feeling I was used to experiencing throughout my life. But something about that physical presence I felt —the convincing that God was real, and that I was receiving a blessing directly from Him— not only did not dissipate after the blessing left, it helped me to look at things from a different perspective. Rather than the normal pessimistic, negative, addict criminal minded, version of myself.

That 'Faith vs fear' concept I mentioned; as mad as I was deep down, as disappointed as I was, I believed it was that little bit of doubt I had in the back of mind. That seed of doubt that was planted that I ultimately believe is what unraveled my blessing. The experts, the non-believers will tell you that it had nothing to do with my doubt. My faith, had nothing to do with the outcome. That my faith, nor my fear can alter outward circumstances. And you know what? They very well could be right. But it doesn't matter. It doesn't matter *to me*.

Because what I look back at, and cherish, in that specific moment, was just that simple shift in my perspective that gave me momentary hesitation to revert back into my old ways. And say *"F this positivity crap it don't work,"* and go right back to getting high, hustling, and heading straight down the same exact path I've headed down my entire life. That's what I wanted to do. I wanted to get out of the quarantine cell, get high, complain, get in a fight, and give up. But just that momentary hesitation, that caused me to think '*You know what? Maybe it was my doubt. Maybe if I would have had more faith it would have went my way. This is still my time. Still my chance*'. Just that change in perspective, was different for me, was a change that needed to change certain parts of who I was. Who I had been. That I could have only gotten from spirituality. Wether you say *"Come on bro, presence of God?! Be realistic"*. That doesn't matter '*to me*'. Whatever the "*facts*" are don't matter to me. I'm not expecting anyone to observe every incident and judge wether it was an act of God. Or measure each sensation you feel to see if you can have a definitive epiphany that can convince you God is real. But there are moments like these in everyones life, where a simple change in perspective could make all the difference in the world. And if spirituality can be the reason your view these occurrences from a different perspective, like it did for me, then that in itself is a good enough reason to believe. Because in that moment, in that tough difficult moment, my spirituality helped me. I needed all the help I can get.

I never did have complete faith. Ever since that moment, I utilize my spirituality, almost in a gamesmanship way; mentally, on a daily basis, to raise my faith above my fear. To have more hope, positivity, optimism, than I do doubt, negativity and pessimism; in order to receive the blessings that God has planned for me and not to miss my blessings like I missed my opportunity to get released early. Which ended up being a blessing in itself. I used the extra time I now had to *re-serve,* to continue to learn and grow. Who knows where I would be if I didn't have an extra 6 months to continue my progess. I thought I was ready to get out. But maybe I wasn't?

It doesn't have to be for a miracle size blessing I'm looking for either. I try to raise my faith above my fear on a daily basis for all things, big and small. For accomplishing creative projects, to difficult work tasks, to just having a good day. Sometimes I use the Bible for inspiration sometimes I use positive self talk but it's all rooted and established in my spirituality. And that's how I use it.

After the counselor took my release date, she told me grab my things. I could head back to general population. But I was not ready for all the crazy ambush of questions and inmates bombarding me asking *"What happened? Why they take your date? Your not going home?"* Instead, I told her I'd stay one more night on 23 hour lockdown with Church. Church was a friend of mine, but I never asked him what his nickname meant. I just assumed it had something to do with the gang he was affiliated to.

When I got back into the quarantine cell, he could see my anger fuming off me, and the first thing he did was look at me, pick up the Bible and he said, *"You know this is why they call me Church right? I really know this shit"*. I knew Church for years. And I had no idea that he got his nickname because of his thorough understanding of the Bible, and his belief in God. And of all the prison cells across the nations bureau of prisons, I happened to be his cellmate, during one of the toughest moments of my life. And of course his name is *'Church'*. This is one of my favorite parts about my spiritual journey.

The first scripture he read was Jeremiah 29:11- *'For I know the plans I have for you. They are plans for good and not for evil, to give you a future and a hope'*. My first scripture ever learned and my all time favorite. The idea of God's plan is the foundation of my faith. In all my spirituality, spiritual beliefs, the idea that there is an established plan for my life constructed by a Power greater than myself, allows me to view my life from a different perspective, and even in that dark moment, when all my natural reflexes tried to convince me this *'Law of Attraction BS is fake'*. That *'God isn't real. F this positivity crap'*. And I wanted to fall back into my old ways and say screw this, those sentences stuck with me. Reminded me that there is a plan for me. A plan for good. Not for evil. So I can't go around doing the same evil things I've done most of my life and live according to God's Plan. That exact scripture is the biggest reason why I don't commit crime at all anymore. It means that much to me. Helped me changed my ways *that* much. I've read the Bible every day since the day I was read that passage.

But I don't read the Bible like a typical religious person or someone with an established religion. Because I don't have any specific religion or religious background. That's not how my spirituality works for me. I read the Bible, treating it like a self-help book, vigilantly scouring, searching for that sentence, that verse, that paragraph to give me that spark inspiration, hope, or guidance to live my day by, my week by, or become my mantra for the month. Or just gain some wisdom or insight through the Bibles numerous life lessons; all which apply to modern day situations explained through parables, and stories, and proverbs that help me develop my wisdom for life. Its another way I practice self-development. I just develop it through spirituality.

———————

Spirituality is believing in something greater than yourself that exists outside of the physical realm. Just to even have that belief, that there's a Higher Power that exists; takes faith. And any person, whoever achieved any success, in any aspect of life, had to have some sort of faith in the that he, or she, would succeed. I'm not saying any faith in particular, in the religious or spirituality realm we're talking about now. I'm sure there's successful people out there that did not believe in any one of these higher powers. I'm talking about a general *belief*. That little word *belief*. A belief in self, belief in a positive outcome, a belief in *you* winning. The problem is we're not all born with this burning belief and faith. And if you're struggling with a drug addiction, or even been through any type of hard times in your life, that faith could easily turn to fear. And that hope, could turn the doubt.

That's why it's important for you to be open minded about learning about a Higher Power. Because if you're one of these people that didn't have the strong belief in self, or that optimism, or that hope, like I was much of my life; each one of the spiritualities that I mentioned have actual scripts, lessons, practices, methods, teachings that deliberately instruct you on '*how*' to develop that belief, that optimism, that hope, and what to do to develop it. God has the Bible, Allah has the Koran, Law of Attraction, the Universe, Source Energy, the 7 Chakras have numerous practices and methods scattered all over all these platforms we use as resources, that will inform you how to develop that belief through whichever specific spirituality. How to *raise* your frequency. *What's frequency?* You can read about it, learn about, and find out how it can help you. Its available for us to use to our advantage.

Spirituality is purely intangible. That means it can't be seen, or touched, or counted. It's the unknown. And the unknown is scary sometimes because we can't see it, or feel it, and we don't actually *know* what it holds for us. But thats where you can stretch, and grow the most. But in the physical realm, the tangible, we know what we're going to get. I can do all the push ups, I can change my diet 1 million times, I can read all I want, but it can only do *so* much. We know what it's going to do. I can only lose so much weight. I can only get so strong. But in the spiritual realm? The possibilities are endless. Its pure abundance. Limitless. This is where you reach those new levels you weren't able to reach on your own. The sense of protection, the peace that comes with the forgiving of your sins, the guidance, the change in your perspective of life, the hope, the optimism, the faith, the trust. Things you cannot buy. Things you cannot force. But these things will help you on a second to second, minute to minute basis, everyday.

Step two, we're opening our mind to a power outside of ourselves. This is where we get the outside help. Where we search for those new levels. Maybe you're not comfortable with the idea of a Higher Power, or you don't like the God word. Maybe its a source of energy that could do it for you; like the Universe, Law of Attraction, or the 7 Chakras. Or even one of the lesser populated religions like Buddhism, Islam, Mormon, etc., that'd you be willing to learn from. You don't even have to necessarily adopt all the theologies and ideals that any one of these suggestions predicate themselves on. You could simply learn from them. Learn from them all if you want. Or maybe you already have a religion. Then that's even better.

The point is, for it to be spirituality that you're comfortable with. The more comfortable you are, the more willing you'd be to learn about it. And if you're learning through spirituality, that means you have *some* faith. And *some* faith is all you need. The more you learn, the more faith you will have. The less doubt, fear, and pessimism you will have. The more your hope and faith will begin to grow. And the more hope and faith you have, the more you will begin to believe in yourself and you'll began see your outward circumstances start to change for the better; right along with that belief.

Hardaway Learning Suggestion:

1. Figure out which Higher Power you are comfortable believing in.

2. Spend 20 minutes a day simply learning about your choice.

3. After learning sufficient enough to have a reasonable grasp on the spirituality choice, pick one or two moments throughout the week to incorporate these beliefs into your everyday life (conceptually or practice wise).

Chapter 3

Step 3: Core Value Lists Practice

Now that we have a base of faith to reinforce our steps in the right direction, we have more to work with. That's what these steps are about. Its about progression and gaining some breathing room. Even if it feels minimal. Even if just a subtle shift in perspective or at the onset of a healthy habit being developed; its enough for our hope to start rising. To have a little more encouragement and be a little more optimistic about our future. We've also learned some so we have more ability and capability. Even if it's just a little bit, that's more than we had and more than enough to work with.

As important as my first positive steps and my spirituality were in my personal transformation, they are foundational steps. Steps to form a base upon what we plan to build ourselves into. There will never be a more important practice that I partook in that helped me build myself into that new person more effectively, more efficiently, and faster, than a practice called a *"Core Value List Practice."* This practice was actually *"how"* I built upon that foundation I illustrated in the previous chapters.

People ask me all the time *"How did you do it?" "How did you get sober?"* And when I'm asked that very broad question, I could say any one of these seven steps because they were all of the upmost importance to me being able to break my cycle of addiction. But my answer is always the same. I say, *"because I worked on myself from the inside-out."* And the way I worked from the inside-out was with a practice called a *"Core Value List Practice."* There was no more important course of action for me than this practice.

One of my favorite quotes of all time is by James Allen, *"Character is not permanent. It is indeed one of the most changeable things in nature, if not changed by the conscious act of will, it is being continually modified and reformed by the pressure of circumstances."*

My entire adult life consisted of bad decisions, big mistakes, negative thoughts, bad luck, big losses that reflected directly in my ever eroding outward circumstances. The worse my drug addiction got, the worst my decisions were. The worse I was; the more I lied, the more I stole, the worse crimes I committed, the more prison time I would have to do when I got caught, the harder it would be to reenter into society, and rectify my life when I got released—and the pressure of the circumstances forced that vicious cycle to repeat itself all of my adult life. Nothing changed. At least not for the better. For the worse it sure did.

I went to jail/prison ten plus times. I got out and relapsed ten plus times. I could try my best to change my number, stay away from so-and-so, find employment, and do the right thing. But as soon as my character flaws (I had developed over years) were triggered, I would slip right back into my old ways. The truth is after that 30-days, 90-days, that year, of being locked away, I was the same person with the same flaws just months or a year later. *I* never changed. So nothing ever changed.

I could try my best to avoid, hold off, and ignore the outward circumstantial pressures, but it was futile because I never changed my inward perception, my core, or my character which controls how you perceive every one of those outward circumstances. So what was the difference between this 56-month federal sentence and the last prison sentence I served, got out, and relapsed after? Outside of the length of the duration, the biggest difference was that I started working on my character. And the core value list practice is how I did it.

I first read about a core value list practice in a book, called **Declutter Your Mind(2)** by S.J Scott and Barrie Davenport. They stated that, *"core values can serve as a measuring stick for all your choices and decisions. Keep you focused on what you want to be in life, and in line with happiness. Clear values, reduces your confusion, over thinking and worry."* Just the title, "Declutter Your Mind" was the whole reason I picked the book up in the first place. I was struggling with concentration, focus and over-thinking, and was looking for a remedy.

It felt like a stretch to think that getting clear on your core values could reduce brain fog. And as much as dumb luck, circumstances, and opportunity, played a part in my transformation, I will always give myself credit for this one major role that I did play. I did sit down with every one of these books, opened them up, and kept a level of open mindedness that they could actually help me. I sat down with this book, with the intention of clearing some brain fog, but I gained so much more from it.

Core Value List Practice

Core values are the fundamental beliefs, characteristics, or traits that a person is known for or operates on. In the book, *Declutter Your Mind,* the author provided a lengthy list of personality qualities and characteristic traits then asked the reader (me), to circle on the list the core values you would like to embody and possess as a person.

While writing this chapter, without the book *Declutter Your Mind* in hand, I simply searched Google for "core value list practice" and a pretty much identical practice popped up with a list of 192 core values from a site called saturdaysgift.com. Here is the link to the practice. You could go there and follow right along step-by-step. https://www.saturdaygift.com/core-values-list/.

You can also search on Google "core value lists practice" and a bunch of similar practices will pop up. They are all one in the same since this is a very common practice. The lists you'll find have every core value, every personality trait, every characteristic that you can think of like:

abundance, affection, discipline, love, focus, fun, spirituality, gratitude, etc. Among the lists, the objection is to circle 10 to 15 of these core values, separate them into life and work categories. And then dwindle them down to your top five in each category: top five for life and top five for work. I still have a copy of my 'top five' lists I made when I did this practice in prison. Here it is.

LIFE   WORK

Conviviality.........Ability

Discipline............Ambition

Enthusiasm..........Composure

Fearlessness..........Diversity

Fun...................Drive

I still remember when I came up with this list. It invigorated me with energy. Just from pure speculation, of the possibility of *being* a person that embodied these traits. Even though it was complete imagination, it filled me with hope. Just the thought of me being this person. It had nothing to do with my circumstances; that I was still sitting in prison and still getting high. It was a look into the future. It was a vision that seemed to part clouds right through everything that I had been through in the past because it had nothing to do with my past.

It enabled me to finally see a different version of myself which was someone I could become, and it gave me an idea. It painted a picture of a different version of myself, and it planted a seed of motivation that sprouted. Even after the next step took a little bit of wind out of my sails. But it was even more important than the first.

After you get clear on the core values that are most important to you, take a sheet of paper out, and write out each core value. For each core value you write down, write a sentence or two about how you are currently living out of alignment with that core value. At this moment, in your life, RIGHT NOW. Currently, how are you *not* this person? Here's an example of my list from my practice.

Ambition: Too much complacency

Composure: Easily overwhelmed

Fun: Always bored

Fearless: Negative thoughts and worries cloud my mind

I did this with every core value on my list and it did sting a little bit but it was necessary. Seeing it on paper—coming from my mind—what I knew about myself. Seeing who I wanted to be gave me inspiration. But then seeing that I wasn't that person *"right now,"* and then seeing *"why"* I'm not that person now, was what I needed. It not only notified me that I had work to do. It made me aware of *what* work I needed to do. This also helped me develop my self-awareness.

Self-awareness is absolutely imperative for any type of change of any form, in any area or facet of life. You must be aware first, that something needs to change, to then do something to change it. It wasn't about a treatment specialist, a counselor, or a parent telling me, *"this is what you need to change. This is who you need to be."* No, it was about my thoughts, a pen and a paper, figuring out myself, what *I* needed to change, about *me*.

The most important thing this practice did for me was help me visualize a different version of myself. Then it laid out a road map of how I could realize that version of myself by highlighting the reasons I wasn't that person now. It started with me thinking of myself in the future using complete imagination. You have to see yourself outside of addiction, you have to see yourself outside of depression, see yourself outside of anxiety; before you can move towards changing it. That is what this practice did for me. It didn't bring me through those obstacles initially. I simply thought around them, and over them, and under them, to seeing myself after those obstacles. It reminded me that I can be that person regardless of what I was struggling with now, or had been through in the past. It reminded me that anyone can be a person with these core values, these characteristics, and these traits. Or whichever ones they choose. You get actually *choose* who you want to be. You have a choice.

This list is meant to be a measuring stick and guide for all your conduct, thoughts, and words. It definitely can be and it should be that, it definitely was for me. But the biggest impact it had on me was, with the utilization of this list, to have a course of action to reform my character; to change who I was, who I had been, and how I thought. The "course of action" part, I did that by creating my own two subsequent steps after my solidified list of most important core values. I put the written down list, into literal action.

———————

The first thing I did with my list of values was go to the dictionary and get the exact definition from the dictionary of the word itself. Doing this gave me a crystal clear picture of what the actual word meant. Of what "*ambitious*" actually means; of what "*discipline*" actually means. For example, the definition of "*discipline*" in the Merriam-Webster Dictionary is "*orderly or prescribed conduct or pattern of behavior.*" I looked it up and wrote down the definition of all my core values. This took out completely any speculation or opinion-based ideas of what it meant to be discipline, fun, ambitious, etc. I erased mentally all the preconceived theories and went solely with the definition. After I got clear on what the values meant, next came the most important step: I put it into action. I started "*acting.*" I started "*being*". And ultimately started "*becoming.*"

After I got the definitions, which was my own personal step, I added another step of my own. Each day, I told myself I would choose one core value to focus on. Just one. And I would spend that day embodying that characteristic. I did this by thinking of practical ways to match my actions with my desired core value. I know you might be thinking *'how would I spend a day being disciplined when I have no discipline?' 'How would I spend the day being fearless when I worry all the time?'* This is a lot easier than it seems but there's no need to overthink it. For one, we have a definition of the characteristic at hand as a starting point. And if you're still having trouble to come up with what to do and how to act out this core value; refer back to your list of sentences you wrote down about how you were out of alignment with that core value, and simply spend the day doing the opposite.

For example, if your core value is "fearless," and your following sentence is *"you worry too much,"* spend that day being aware of your thoughts, recognizing when you worry, and flipping the thought to a less worrisome thought. Just by doing this, you are actively rewiring your brain and unraveling old mental habits. These are the steps we need. Specifically, I remember doing this with one of my core values, "conviviality" which is; *"the quality of being friendly and lively and friendliness."* I wrote how I, myself, was out of alignment with conviviality; *"don't talk to a lot of people, don't smile, and don't socialize."* On that day that I chose to focus on conviviality. I set my daily goal to go hold conversations with three people that

I rarely talked to in the unit housing. I also made a conscious effort to smile, even if for no reason.

"Honesty" was another core value that was important to me. Mostly because being dishonest was such a glaring regretful characteristic I developed over the years of addiction. Big lies, small lies, creative lies, stupid lies; I was living a lie. On the day I chose to focus on "honesty," I would simply be honest the entire day. No exaggerations and no white lies. Complete transparency and truthfulness. I was actually surprised how easily it came to just *be honest*. Now never telling a lie won't keep me sober for the rest of my life, but I did utilize my core value list to improve on a weakness. It did make feel like a better person with higher morals and integrity. That was an improvement for me and it gave me a boost of confidence.

Generosity also became a focal point to me. That day when being "generous" was the focus, anybody that literally asked me for anything, or mentioned they needed something, I would give it to them. Just for one day. I was even generous with my time. Roaming the unit looking for anyone struggling with their treatment work until I stumbled across a friend with English as a second language, and found myself an hour in, missing my scheduled basketball show, holding back frustration and putting on a fake smile. I wasn't all the way there yet. But you can't expect to be. However, I was taking steps toward being that "generous" person I wanted to be and that's what it's about; getting out of your comfort zone, reversing some of those old character flaws, and planting seeds for new ones. Leaving the cell, my friend gave me a big hug and a smile and said, "Bro thank you so much. I really needed your help." That made me feel good. Not only because I was generous and helped someone, but because I also accomplished a personal goal. And that's another part of this.

The joy of accomplishment is one of the greatest feelings to experience. But you have to have goals or objectives to actually accomplish to enjoy this feeling of accomplishment. These goals are easy goals to accomplish because they don't have to be hard. They can be flexible, free, and all up to you. Set your goal every day to personify one of these core values. If you choose "fun," spend the day *doing* something fun. Make an appoint to *have* fun. If you choose "discipline," just for one day, you've got a stick to your diet, your routine and your workout. Just today, and your goal is accomplished.

I did this consciously for couple months, then I started thinking differently. If I could stay disciplined, be enthusiastic, not worry, be creative, and socialize, for one day;

why not two days? Why not a week? If I could pick one core value to focus on, why not two.? Why not three? And that's what this practice did for me. For all the benefits; easily accomplished goals, the introspection, self-aware-ness, for the vision of the future. All benefits which I reaped. Nothing compares to the impact it had on me as a man in the reforming of my character. Because with every day, every thought, and every act I was actively *being* a different person. Therefore, I was actually *becoming* a dif-ferent person.

These traits that I had my whole life, that I had devel-oped during my criminal days and my drug addictions were part of who I was. I had believed they were perma-nent. That they were just *"who I was"* and that they were part of my character. That's why I love the James Allen's quote that I mentioned at the beginning so much *"char-acter is not permanent."* I thought I was born lazy with no discipline. I thought I would always have doubt and fear. Like I would always be pessimistic. I stayed that way because that's what I thought about myself and that's part of the reason that's how I always acted. I never tried to change it because I didn't think that I could.

The more I acted out these core values in my daily life, the acts and deeds acted as seeds that grew into my character. You don't even necessarily have to *do* the entire core value list practice. Simply look at your character as a whole. Who are you now? I'm not talking about your circumstances. I mean your *being*. Your personality. Who are you at your core? Who would you like to be? Who would you like to *not* be? We all don't want to be addicted, or depressed, or anxious. But maybe its one of these characteristics that's been part of who you are that has been innately tied tightly to your addictive nature— that if you changed— could help you change the part of you that's kept you addicted. Our character is who we are. And as character changes, you're changing as a person. My character was what I needed to change to change my life.

Generosity, kindness, discipline, fun, ambition, and ability have nothing to do with drug addiction. But by working from the inside-out, the person I was inside changed, and I could see the difference in how I reacted to inward tendencies and perceived my outward circumstances. And I remember it like it was yesterday the exact moment when I realized that.

———————————

Walking down the unit hallway in prison after months of core value practice, on top of my daily reading, workout routines, and other healthy habits, I actually did have a new glow to me. People actually noticed. They gave me compliments. I felt *different*. I felt *better*. I could actually *feel* it. Notice it. I was aware that I was in a good mood. I couldn't point to a single moment in the past six years where I could say, without a doubt, that I was in a good mood at *that* period of time. But times had changed.

I hadn't been high in two months, hadn't even thought about getting high. Thats when I walked past the cell of one of my old get high buddies in prison. He called me into his cell. «Hey Skinny, you trying to get high?" Out of pure reflex, not even a thought crossed my mind, I chuckled and said, "no bro, I'm good but thank you." I laughed. He was taken back and said, "What do you mean? You don't have to pay for it, it's free." Again. I laughed and said "Thanks bro, but I'm good." And I was thankful. There was a time in my life where being offered free drugs would have made my day. This was not that time.

Not realizing what I just did, I made it back to my cell, sat down, looked out the window into the blue sky and about 90 seconds later, it hit me like a ton of bricks. '*What the fuck did I just do? Did I just turn down free drugs?!*' Never can I recall, ever, turning down a free high in my entire life. I sat there, staring out the window for about five minutes with the biggest smile that ever graced my face thinking, '*wow I cannot believe this stuff really works. I'm really on to something.*' It was the first time in a decade plus, that I actually felt like the tables (Me vs. my addiction) had finally turned in my favor. Out of all the moments and realizations in my 33 years of life; that just might be my favorite.

It was too late for my old demons to resurface and me to revert back into my old ways. In fact, I've never been high anytime after that moment. I put in the necessary effort to convert those old ways into new ways. I had changed. It started with a vision of the future. Thought up out of complete imagination, that proceeded with actions, that took route inside of me, that sprouted into new character. We've all heard the famous quote by Lao Tzu, "*watch your thoughts; they become words. Watch your words; they become actions. Watch your actions; they become habits. Watch you habits; they become character.*" A quote proved true time and time again, through a disastrous 14-year stretch of my life riddled with prison and addiction. I couldn't escape it. But guess what? I acted out the same principle, in real life this time, from a positive standpoint rather than negative, and the quote again was proven true. This time it worked for my advantage. And I changed. My thoughts changed, my words changed, my actions changed, my habits changed, and my character changed. Then my life changed for the better.

Hardaway Learning Suggestion:

1. Google "Core Value List Practice." Thousands of results will pop up. Find a site that provides the instructions that you feel comfortable with and follow along.

   *Two Good practices I found online:

   https://www.saturdaygift.com/core-values-list/

   https://www.berkeleywellbeing.com/core-values.html

2. Choose your top ten core values you would like to embody as a person (top five for personal and top five for work).

3. Get out a sheet of paper and a pen then write out a sentence or two about how you are currently out of alignment with each core value.

4. Jot down the dictionary's definition of each core value.

5. Think of practical ways you can "act" out these core values throughout the days and be aware of actions that are not conducive to personifying this core value.

6. Everyday, focus solely on one core value and make it your focus. Focus on one core value every day for two to four weeks or until you feel comfortable with focusing on two core values a day.

Chapter 4

Step 4: Start Learning Again

We have a foundation that we're building upon and we're building it from the inside-out. The development of the first three steps will always be an ongoing process. Undoubtedly, for that process to continue, you have already been doing a lot of what the fourth step is predicated on. And that's to "*Start Learning Again.*"

-There's no doubt that in order to take your first positive steps; you had to learn. To form a sense of spirituality; you had to learn. You even had to learn how to do a core value list practice. You've learned in all these steps and will continue to learn in the steps after this. But in step four, we're going to take a different direction, a specific direction, and again its all up to you.

Think about it. What signifies your ascension from childhood to adulthood? It starts with our entry into grade school, where we are expected to take classes and courses to form a fundamental base of knowledge sound enough to move into the next grade. Then to junior high. Then to high school. Then possibly to college. To reach the next level of adolescence, you have to learn. This is the same process for most humans on the planet because it is *that* important. What you learn and what you know determines how much you grow. To be an astronaut, a business owner, a mogul, an artist, an entertainer, an entrepreneur, an influencer, or whatever you want to be, at any age or stage in your life, you have to develop some sort of knowledge to climb that success latter in any field.

That process is going to be no different for us trying to climb out of addiction. To continue moving forward, we're leaving our addiction and looking forward to realizing new aspirations. In this step, we're going to learn things that are going to help us insure that progress. But unlike grade school or high school we're not taking a bunch of courses that formulate the general consensus of education. We're going to expand our knowledge with a specificity that has nothing to do with anything *but* the person that we plan to become.

———————————

I know this is not the case for everybody, but I probably forgot 80% of what I learned in high school. Outside of your basic reading, writing, and math skills, I couldn't tell you one thing from those advanced placement classes I participated in through high school. This is not a knock on the education system because although I might have forgot a lot of the material, the process of learning is pre-eminent to any kind of development. So during that time, I was learning. I was growing. When I got expelled from high school, became a felon, couldn't play college football because of the legal issues, and turned to the streets; I stopped learning. I also stopped growing. I believe the two had a lot to do with each other.

Another reason why a lot of the curriculum went in one ear, and out the other, is because it didn't have anything to do with who I wanted to become as a person (the fact that I didn't know who I wanted to be or become at that age was big reason why). But if I wanted to be a chemist, I'm sure that chemistry class would've helped me and a lot of the material I learned in that class I would have retained.

But that's not the case. And we're going to have to make sure that doesn't happen here. If you're old enough to read this book, then you're old enough to think of specific directions that you can apply your learning capabilities, to expand your knowledge, and to heighten your abilities.

Learning was so vital on my journey from addiction to sobriety. It was actually my personal *"Step One."* My *"Any Positive Step in The Right Direction'"*was actually *learning.* I started learning through reading self-help books, to learn how to become a better person. We can all agree that learning how to be a better person can help you in a variety of ways in all aspects of your life. That's a good example of the type of learning that we're going to go forward with in this process.

So, what kind of learning am I speaking of exactly? If you've read the previous chapters, you notice the apparent flexibility with the guidelines of each step I present. It is intended to be that way. But where this specific step differs from the previous steps and the steps after this, is it has the option to actually stray away from the traditional self development route the other steps are predicated on. Of course, you can *"learn"* how to become a different, better, person. You *can* learn that. I did. Find ways to rise to to higher levels of morality, and ascend to new heights of character. And I'm here to say that very well might be the best way to proceed in this step. But this step has the variable of also having a horizontal expansion approach. To widen your horizons. To spread your web of knowledge in any area you feel will benefit you.

Maybe you're like me, and your first steps were to read self-help books, and now you're on step four. Well, I never did stop learning about how to become a better person. And that journey continues. But as I continued to grow, I decided to expand my knowledge in other areas of life that would benefit my overall ability to advance my *actual* life. These are the type of intellectual gains that prompted me to incorporate this as a step, as an integral part of my transformation from addiction to sobriety.

In prison, I was enrolled in an electrician apprenticeship program much of my sentence. I had aspirations to seek employment in the trade when I got released. I decided to take it upon myself to further my education, to enhance my capabilities in the field that I planned to pursue when I got released. So every day, on top of my workout, on top of my reading, I set aside 30 minutes a day to go over the electric code handbook just to learn. Just to sharpen my skills.

Now being an electrician has nothing to do with getting, or staying sober. But when the covid restrictions were lifted, and after months of studying over the electricians handbook, I went back to work in the apprenticeship program; and I did feel more comfortable. I did feel more capable. I did feel more competent. That gave me a boost of confidence that I really needed. That confidence helped me in other areas of my life. Like my mood, and my stress levels. That's because I got better and improved from what I had learned.

Later, I even carved out 30 more minutes slot into my routine to try and learn the Spanish language. Being completely foreign it kept me mentally stimulated, and it was fun. It was also challenging. It gave me a vessel to push myself. Just to see myself learn certain words, be able to read sentences out of a book, gave me a sense of accomplishment. Just to be able to understand Spanish in that little bit of capacity, made me that much more knowledgable, and you never know when it could come in handy. It didn't cost me nothing but a little bit of time, but that knowledge is part of who I am now.

Maybe you don't want to be electrician or speak Spanish. Perhaps you want to start a business. Take some time out of the day to learn through books, YouTube, a podcast about what it would take to start a business. To get funding to start a business. The logistics of your business. Take notes, pay attention and learn about it. Even if you don't know what kind of business you want to start. Or perhaps you *do* know what kind of business you want to start. A clothing line, a hair salon, a barber shop, life coaching business, a restaurant, an e-commerce store. Take some time to learn about the ins and outs of that industry.

The most effective form of learning for this step, and really in general, is intellectual gain that fully aligns with your purpose and the aspirations you have. If you don't know your purpose, or even where to start; trust me I've been there. But the sooner you figure this out —what you want to do, what you want to be, what you believe your purpose is, the direction you want to take your life— the better. Then the sooner you can start building towards that.

Thinking of what our purpose is, believing what it is, knowing exactly what we want to do with our lives, at any age, can be overwhelming to think about at times. Even discouraging. Thats because we tend to look at our dreams from the perspective of *'why it wont work'*, instead of *'why it will work'*. We look at our circumstances, our finances, our position in life, our addiction, our depression, our motivation, our skills and convince ourselves that these possibilities that lie in the future, are too far out of reach. Like we're washed up, its too late, we're too old, that it can't happen. Instead, get a vision for the future. The future that you desire, regardless of any circumstance. Use your imagination. If money, time, effort, luck, and not a single other obstacle lied in your way to living the life of your dreams, what would you be? What would you want to be? What would you want to spend your life doing? What would make you happy? What does your gut tell you? A lot of times, with all those obstacle cleared from your sight, your gut will give you a clear vision of your purpose. And in reality, its not as farfetched as you might think. Especially when you can study, and grow, and learn how to become that person.

Even if you are not 100% sure on what you want you future to look like, as long as the direction you choose to take your learning capabilities in, is a positive one, the trajectory for your growth will be on an incline. And if what you believed to be your purpose at the beginning, changes in a month, or 6 months, or a year, that's okay. Because your purpose might still be somewhere along that trajectory. Maybe to the upper left, or upper right. But as long as *upward* is the trajectory, you're moving in the right direction. That knowledge that you gained could very well be applicable to your new found purpose. It also could have been what you needed to learn to *bring* you to your newfound purpose.

When I believed my purpose was to be a high rolling drug dealer, and I was trying to learn new ways to hustle. New ways to get money. That was the trajectory I was on. Unremittingly downtrodden. It led me to want to be a scammer and a thief. Other downward trajectories. My life followed that trajectory accordingly. Rapid decline, in spiral fashion. It had everything to do with what I was attempting to learn. What I was feeding my mind and spirit.

On the flip side, when I began learning about ways to "*cope with stress,*" I learned about a tool called *journalling*. Me *learning* about how to cope with stress, brought me to this journalling. I practiced it, and noticed that I could go hours just journalling, and writing, clear minded, fully submerged in that elusive "*zone'.*" It was a good feeling. I continued to experiment with my writing eventually writing 3 books. One of them your reading *right now.* A book that falls directly in line with what I believe my purpose is. But I would have never found this segment of my purpose had I never decided to *learn* about ways to cope with stress. It was the growth through learning that brought me to this part of my purpose.

But maybe you don't know what you want to do, what your purpose is, and don't even want to think about it right now; that's fine too. Maybe you just wanna progress. Progress will bring you closer to figuring that out. There are so many ways that we can expand our knowledge, sharpen our skills, and enhance our overall capabilities from learning. Maybe you'd like to be financially literate? You can learn about the stocks, investing, etc.; so you can be smarter with your money. Or perhaps you have weaknesses you'd like to strengthen; learning how to cope with anxiety, depression, anger, etc. There are books and blogs and YouTube pages dedicated to teaching ways to cope with all of these things. You can learn about.

I could go on and on about the types of learning we could do, what you can learn about, but we all know what learning is about. We all know how to do it. In this step, other than the adequate requisite time and effort needed to learn; there are two real parameters to go about it:

Number one: It must be beneficial to you.

Number two: It has to be something you want to learn about and you will enjoy learning about.

It being beneficial, meaning that its contributing to the advancement in your knowledge in ways that will actually benefit you in your every day life. That can *help* you in your every day life. That's why, when I stated learning, I started learning how to be more *optimistic*. It really helped me change aspects of how I was living by changing my perspective to a more hopeful, positive, faithful outlook, which were all useful perspectives for me in my every day life. If you learn how to bake cookies, you will know how to bake cookies, but it's not gonna help you grow as a person. Unless you want to be a baker.

The second thing is; it *has* to be something that you *want* to learn about, and will *enjoy* learning about. Like the previous steps, what you learn about is up to you. But don't make this some arduous task, feel like a duty, an obligation, or a job. But if its necessary for you to learn, at least make sure you're interested in the topic and enjoy learning about it. This is key for one big reason: *so that you keep doing it! So that you keep learning*'! The last thing you want to do, is keep doing something, that's not fun and uninteresting.

But its appropriate for me to mention, if the information is absolutely necessary for you to understand, and its not necessarily *enjoyable,* and will benefit you, there's no harm in learning about it. As long as you can maintain your persistence and consistency long enough to comprehend the information, it will help you regardless. Even if it is boring. That's where learning in small time increments can help. When I got released from prison, and pursued my electrician career, and a couple months into the job I had a mishap that shutdown half the buildings electricity, shutting down production for hours, scared me to death, had me walking around with egg on my face for a week, and indefinitely reversed my aspirations to become an electrician; I wouldn't dare pick up another electrician handbook. Because its so boring and I don't need the knowledge. Currently I spend 30 minutes a day learning on YouTube ranging from different topics like: *'How to build business credit'. 'How to self-publish a book'.* Its not fun, but I do need the info. 30 minutes a day, on Youtube that's how I learn today. And wouldn't you know it? I learned how to self-publish an entire book from learning on YouTube.

Wether you want to take some online courses, simply read books, or find other ways to learn on your own; learning is an essential component of growth. Its going expand our mind, outside of those close confines that addiction has limited our minds to, and get our brains back working again. Get the juices flowing. Get the gears turning. At the same time, we're sharpening our skills, gaining wisdom and enhancing our capabilities. The more capable you are, the more likely you are to succeed. The more able you are, the more confident you will feel, and the better off you'll be. This step, unlike the other 6 steps, isn't necessarily focused directly at the root problem, which, of course, is our addiction. What you learn, what you decide to learn, could very well be something that will benefit you more, once you've overcome your addiction. But that's the exact point. You will overcome your addiction. There's not a fiber in my body that thinks that overcoming any obstacle, including a drug addition is insurmountable. That's why we have to keep preparing ourselves as if that day is going to come. Because it will. Learning is all about preparing. You don't learn how to create content on social media and instantly became an influencer. Or learn a computer skill and be a master. Or learn about crypto and become a billionaire. Or read an electrician handbook and instantly become a journeyman. But your building towards something. Preparing.

I 100% gained employment when I was released from prison because of that electrical experience I was able to put on my resume from what I learned about the trade on my free time when I was incarcerated. That employment helped me avoid some of the pitfalls I fell into after my past stints of being locked up and then being released; no money, no income, no car, no clothes. What I learned, made me more capable to be able handle some of these adverse situations life tends to continually throw at you. Not to handle them from a mentality standpoint as far as managing internal turbulence(although I did *learn* how to do that as well), but from an external standpoint. I was more fit, and suitable to approach these external occurrences than I was in my past attempts to reenter society. Giving me a much better chance to succeed and stay sober *this* time, than the *last* time. That's because *this* time, I was better. That's why learning is not just the most effective way to expand your capabilities and grow.; its the ONLY way.

Hardaway Learning Suggestion:

1. Search your desires for what you believe you'd consider to be your purpose.

2. Think of a skill, a base of knowledge, or information that could bring you closer to realizing that purpose.

3. Spend 30-minutes a day learning about the topic.

Second Option

1. Think of a skill, or skillset, that could benefit you in any way. Personal or Aspiration wise.

2. Spend 30-minutes a day learning about it.

Chapter 5

Step 5: Focusing on "The Body" and "The Mind"

In the previous steps, we focused mostly internally. Developing inner qualities such as knowledge and learning. Even more intangible gains like character and spirituality. In step five, we're going to take a different approach, and focus our attention and energy on the physical; on our body and our mind.

I'm sure the first thing that comes to your mind when you hear *"focusing on your body,"* is exercise. Although I do believe exercise is one of the most effective tools to transform one's mind and body, and was my personal "step five," and remains a key factor in my journey from addiction, and contributes to my ability to remain sober; it is not the end all be all. There are so many practices and directions you can go to move toward in this step to focus on your mind and your body. And several of them we already know about.

Examples for body: Exercise, yoga, diet, intermittent fasting, vitamin supplements

Examples for mind: Meditation, visualization, breath work, vitamin supplements, yoga, nature walks

You can choose any one of these choices, or the many more that I'm sure I left off this list because there are just so many options. And there are equally, if not more, benefits to all these practices. They each bring something different to the table.

Notable Benefits:

- Meditation: Relaxation, lower blood pressure, Anxiety control, controlling thoughts

- Yoga: Flexibility, muscle strength and tone. Protection from injury, peacefulness

- Intermittent fasting: Organ health, weight loss, detoxes body, supports immune health

- Visualization: Boost confidence, reduce anxiety

- Breath work: Anxiety control

- Exercise: Overall health, bone, muscle, body strength, cardiovascular health

Focus less on the six examples of practices I just presented because there are many more than those six. Instead focus more on the variety of benefits each practice brings to the table. Each one of these practices, that can fall into this category of "mind and body" can bring different benefits that we look to incorporate into to our lives. That's the goal in this step. Its no different from the benefits we looked to gain from the previous steps. Just a different way to go about it.

Almost every one of these practices I've listed above I incorporate in my daily routine currently, or have tried some point during my journey from addiction to sobriety. But when I was in your shoes, just trying to progress, and figure out where to start. I began with the most obvious choice. More than likely the one that comes to mind first, when you think of focusing on your physical body. The choice that I believe is the most beneficial. That of course, is: *exercise.*

Exercise, fitness, and working out, has innumerable benefits like: cardiovascular health, stress relief, weight loss, and strength training. It also gives you a boost of dopamine which is very important for those struggling with, or recovering from an addiction, because your dopamine levels are depleted so badly during drug abuse. When I actually began my first workout routines, I was actually in the middle of my last withdrawal period I've ever had in my life. I managed to muster up enough energy to drag my self through a 20-minute workout. And when I got going, sweating, and my heart rate rose, I couldn't feel any part of the withdrawal I had been feeling five minutes before. I know for a fact it helped me overcome that particular series of withdrawals, which we all know can be quite brutal.

I have experienced all the mentioned benefits plus many more. Getting in good shape helped me with my confidence, boosted my self-esteem, and is a healthy productive habit. Those are all pluses. We need all the pluses we can get. I could go on and on about the benefits of exercise but I won't because this book is not dedicated towards the specifics of any *one* practice. But it is dedicated to revelations and the realizations I've come across through my journey from addiction to sobriety. One of those revelations came in a beneficial life lesson that I learned through my fitness journey. And that lesson was about: *results.*

––––––––––––––––

I was sitting in prison still getting high. I was also also getting fat. I was up to 240lbs. Keep in mind that my street/prison nickname was "Skinny." My whole life I'd been a skinny, scrawny kid. But now I was the opposite. At this point, a continued addiction and weight gain were clear negatives. I had already begun the process of my transformation (although I didn't know it at the time) of becoming a better version of myself by partaking in my personal *"step one." "Any step in the right direction,"* which for me, was reading self-help books. So despite the overeating, the weight gain, and the continued drug use I had that developed a subtle mentality shift. A shift in open-mindedness and some optimism, which was all I needed to prompt me to start a simple, basic by all measures, 20-minute workout routine from Monday through Friday. I didn't jump in the circuit with the 1,000 pushup-a-day crew. Or start running ten miles a day. No. I just started small. BUT I did start.

When I was the best high school athlete in the state of Alaska in football, not one time did I ever try to improve through a commitment to training. This is the fastest and most surefire way to improve in athletics. But I didn't even bother. I was lazy in that regard. I never had the discipline or the persistence to see the results. Without results I had no motivation. Without motivation I practically never worked out in my entire life. Even though I had every necessity to train given the fact I had aspirations to play college football I needed to prepare for. But I was always good enough to be the best wide receiver in the state; so that was good enough for me. That was my mentality.

And while I was an addict? Don't even get me started. I was not in the business of improving my life. And of course my life continued to get worse. I was never even open minded enough to think about, or try a workout routine. Some of that is because I had no previous evidence that *it could* help me, because I never had seen any results. The rest had to do with the fact that I was still lazy, undisciplined, and unwilling. So I never tried. I never helped my self. And I stayed stuck.

But in that cell, working out for 20 to 30 minutes a day, for about three weeks, with my cellmate right along with me motivating me, my old tendencies began to rear they're ugly head. I would look in the mirror, look sideways, flex, and I couldn't see the results. That old quitter inside of me, that no-discipline, lazy mentality told me '*F this shit. This shit don't work.*' But then I got lucky. The three weeks of working out were during an institutional lockdown in which I had no access to the recreation yard. Meaning, I had no access to a weight scale. I was judging my progress by looking in the mirror and seeing if I could see the six pack, looking if I could see my muscles. But I couldn't. I was ready to give up. Then out of the blue, the yard opened up. The first thing I wanted to do was hop on the scale and see if my hard work has paid off. And I'll tell you right now with 100% certainty; if my hard work hadn't paid of, there would be no more working out for me and I would have missed out on piece of my life that has helped me change it so drastically.

You can put two and two together and come to the conclusion given the fact that I was an addict, and a criminal, that I was much more into instant gratification, than the slow and steady, persistent route to realize my results. Do the crime, get the money, NOW. '*Screw working a job and waiting two weeks for a paycheck.*' '*Forget learning how to work through my problems, change my mentality, and overcome my struggles.*' Get high, ignore them, NOW. I wasn't into delayed gratification. *Which is* fitness. Patience, persistence, consistency; all important virtues to embody, but all dyer weaknesses for me before addiction and they worsened while an addict. But I have improved a lot in those ares. And my fitness journey is responsible for the majority of my progress in those areas.

When I got to the yard, the first thing I did was hop on the scale. My eyes lit up. It said 228lbs! I went from 240lbs to 228lbs in three weeks and a lightbulb flipped on inside of me. My hard work *HAD* payed off.

See, it never mattered one bit how many times I looked in the mirror or if I had a scale in my cell that I could hop on every day to check my weight. That would have never changed one thing about the outcome of me seeing my desired results. All that mattered, was that I stuck with it and I did the workout. That I did the work and that is exactly what I did do. I did do that. I did the push-ups, the squats, the sit ups. As basic as it was, as slow as the pace, it didn't matter. That's all I ever had to do to get my results. And I did get my results. I went at my own pace. I didn't compare myself to nobody. I didn't jump off and go straight to the maximum advanced mode. No. I just worked my way up, started basic and slow, but most importantly, I stuck with it.

Those results really motivated me. It motivated me to continue. But if I would've never stuck with a long enough to see those results, I never would've found that motivation. That motivation that I gained that day, from that time period sticks with me to this day. I know for a fact, that if I show up to the gym, workout, put the effort in, I will (not maybe) see my results. I've never looked back on my fitness and that was a benefit that changed my life. That goes for every one of these practices, in every one of these steps. That goes for whichever specific practice, method, or exercise you choose to do, in *this* step; step five. The results you desire, you will achieve, if you stick with it. I learned that about life, in *this* step.

Let me take you back to step two: spirituality. That was us seeking gains from the outside physical realm. In the unseen. Progress in areas you can't necessarily see, or touch. Progress for the most part, is intangible. Which is critical to growth. But step five is the opposite. We *are* looking for that tangible progress that we can see and feel. It's about us being well-rounded and balanced in our approach to improve and become this better version of ourselves.

When I was running the streets addicted to heroin and meth, eating fast food every day for months or not eating for three days at any given week; was that the reason I was addicted? No. Did it help me? No. Well we don't need things that don't help us. Now that I'm sober and I eat clean; does that keep me healthy and in shape? Yes. Does that help me? Yes. And we need all the help we can get.

Would working out during my addiction have instantly snapped me back into sobriety? Maybe not. But being persistent to an exercise routine, did get me in shape, and did fill my day with a positive productive habit. It also boosted my confidence and it was essential to me building my first sign of discipline that I've ever had in my life. I needed to find some discipline somehow, and I ended up finding some through fitness. That little bit of discipline I built upon has helped me in all aspects of my life, including getting sober.

We can't control everything. A lot of what it takes to get and remain sober happens internally; from perspective shifts, character development, will, and discipline. But it is hard to control how long progress in those areas will take to make, because it's different for everybody, and its harder to judge.

This step is about externally, and most of all of that we can control, and the benefits are just as impactful and abundant. We can control what we eat, we can control whether or not we workout, we can control if we do yoga, breath work, meditate, take vitamin supplements, or go on nature walks. This isn't about figuring out *"how to"* because much of what this step pertains, we already know *"how to."* You just do it. That's is why it's important to remember that all of these options are available to you at this step.

Sure, fitness is world renowned for its benefit and has benefited me beyond measure, but maybe you can't even fathom trying to motivate yourself to start a workout routine. Or its just straight up ain't your thing. That's the case for a lot of people. People who aren't even struggling with an addiction. There's nothing wrong with that and if its not your thing, that's fine. But if you're capable of searching on YouTube something like "ten minute basic yoga", and doing one of the routines five times a week in the morning, there's no doubt that it will help your physical health. You'll feel looser instantly. You'll feel calmer instantly. You'll *feel* it. The feeling of improved physical health will improve your life. Period. This step is about taking vitamins, and *feeling* better. Meditating and *feeling* more relaxed. Working out and *feeling* stronger.

Most of all these examples mentioned in this chapter, are key components to my daily routine and maintaining my sobriety. Meditation and yoga are a big part of my morning routine, and I honestly feel more clear minded and focused when I make an appoint to practice them. I

take vitamin supplements 5- HTP, L-Theanine and vitamin D, everyday for mood health, and natural B vitamins
3, 6, and 12, from a scoop of nutritional yeast for energy,
daily. I've been intermittent fasting for about three years
now which keeps my weight under control. When I for-
mulated my diet, I literally searched Google "b*est foods
for depression" and "b*est food for brain fog."* I eliminated
foods that caused brain fog and stress because I needed
help in those areas. I made a clean, strict diet and started
eating healthy, and found that when I stray away from
that organic-based diet, areas in my life such as; fatigue,
sleep, and concentration seem to suffer.

Now none of these things have anything to do with
getting, or remaining sober, but progress in these adjacent
areas will make you that much more suitable and that much
better. And the better you are, the better chance you have
of getting and remaining sober. Mood, sleep, concentration, energy; improvements in these areas equal improvements across the board. We need all the improvements we
can get. Focusing your attention on your physical body
and mind, is a way to balance our approach in our progress so we're not solely reliant upon learning, spirituality,
or any other one thing.

There are countless ways to focus on improving your
physical body and your mind. Some I mentioned. Some

I'm sure I forgot. Nature walks, stretching, yoga, meditation, vitamins, diet, drink, water, healthy sleep routine, etc. Even thinking outside the box like therapy or counseling. Both great for mental health. There's also a new type of treatment in the field of Functional Medicine that focuses on hormones, detoxification, toxic metal detox, and neurofeedback, to name a few. I actually do neronfeedback therapy once a week and have experienced significant benefits with reducing brain fog. Or maybe it can be a subtraction rather than an addition; like no more fast food or no more alcohol. Think of ways that you could focus on your mind or body. Pick one area to focus on. One practice, one method, and roll with it.

It's important to note that this is about action rather than thought. Continuous action. Whatever practice, method, or exercise we partake in, we want to add into our routine. We want to do it, and keep doing it. That way we can maximize our results, build discipline, and that'll also be another healthy habit added to our repertoire. My favorite part about this step is you don't have to think, assess, or judge whether or not it's working, or if you're making progress. No. You'll be able to *see* it. You'll be able to *feel* it. You'll be able to take the vitamins and *feel* the energy. You'll be able to hop on the scale and *see* the numbers reduce. Take your shirt of *see* your muscles. Take a selfie while your at it; why not? Because whatever practice you choose, if you stick with it, the results are not up for debate. They are not mere possibilities. They are guarantees. You are guaranteed to see results. And those results are going to motivate you to do more.

Hardaway Learning Suggestion:

1. Search Youtube for "Basic full body 20-minute workout." Hundreds of results will appear.

2. Try a new full body work out every other day for two to four weeks until you feel comfortable working out five days a week or increasing workout duration by 15-minutes.

Option Two

1. Incorporate 10-minutes of mental exercise a day i.e. meditation, visualization, breathe work

Option Three

1. Identify an area where you might be struggling mentally or physically i.e. fatigue, anxiety, depression, focus, high blood pressure, etc.

2. Search Google for "Vitamin supplements for [said deficiency].

3. Incorporate supplements into your daily regimen.

Chapter 6

Step 6: Do More

Step six is a simple one: Do More. Step six, by all rights, is identical to step one in the sense that the responsibility is on you to search your desires and rely on yourself to choose the direction you want to take in this step. It is another '*any step in the right direction*'. Just like step one, it is without any of the categorical parameters the other steps have in place like: spirituality, learning, core values, mind, and body. It is purposely vague and open-ended because we know ourselves best, and one of the suggestions and methods in these other steps might have produced more results than the others. But that's how life works in general and it's not a bad thing. Some things are for us, some things are not. Some things work, some things don't.

Through all these steps—one through five—we are essentially in the *trying* stage. We don't actually know what works. We're actually trying to figure out what it is that works for us. At this point we'll have a better understanding of exactly what that is and that's why "Do More" is at the latter stage of this process.

Maybe it was step two and your outlook on spirituality that opened your mind and your eyes to a new way of living and you're open minded to doing more? So on top of your daily Bible study, you add deep prayer or a daily online sermon. Or you go in a completely different direction and look to learn more about Source Energy, the Universe, or Chakras. Maybe working on core values really improved your character so you've got your five main core values that you focus on, but you want to do more and be more direct so you can focus specifically on different aspects of your life? You then divide your life into five main categories: work, relationships, leisure, travel, and finance. You pick five more specific core values to fall into those categories and start improving on those specific areas. Or when you started learning again? That step for you was learning about financial literacy and the stock market peaked your interest. Or are you choosing to learn another language and feel comfortable adding 30 more minutes on top of your study session? Perhaps when you focus your attention on the physical body through fitness, you seen results, but you want to see more; so you add a diet on top of the workout to increase your results. These are all simple, straightforward, easy to understand examples of "doing more." That's this step.

It's also highly possible that it's something that has nothing to do with any of the steps I mentioned or didn't even say a word about in this entire book, but you've always wanted to try or you think it will help you. Go for it; therapy, NA meetings, AA meetings, or as far as going to treatment. One where you could get professional care and continue some of the practices you've learned in the previous step; that could be a step you take. Any type of self-help or self-improvement method is available to you in this step. Pick one you like best and roll with it. This is us brainstorming, starting from scratch, trying to figure out ways to get better, and to improve. Just like step one, the similarities are exact except for one massive glaring discrepancy that will make all the difference when we start doing more, and that is: that we know more than we did at the beginning, thus, making us more suitable to do more.

The reason "Do More" is step six—and after five subsequent steps—is because at this stage in the process, if adequate effort was asserted and persistence was practiced, there is absolutely no doubt that you have gained from what you learned and partook in during those steps. Whether it be emotional, mental, physical, intellectual, or spiritual; or from a perspective standpoint or mentality shift. A character upgrade in optimism, self-love, positivity, a full-blown awakening, or an improvement in any other way, shape or form that takes place. Just that little bit of improvement, no matter how sizable, is what makes us more capable than we used to be, which counts for a whole lot when you take on the challenge of starting to do more.

Doing more can sound intimidating. In fact, 50% of these motivational gurus will tell you *"do more, be relentless, and never quit."* And we all know that works. It's effective but the truth is that mindset can be awfully difficult to just muster up out of thin air. Not all of us have that kind of determination just sitting inside of us waiting to be summoned up at the snap of a finger. Especially when we first decide to start our process of change. I know I didn't have it within me initially. I had to rely on steady progression. The tangible and intangible progress that I saw in each intended direction were the results that formed my motivation to persist and proceed, and to explore new ways. It is about getting that concrete evidence, that *this* learning I'm doing, *this* spiritual growth, *this* exercise, that *these* steps are actually helping. And with that realization, I was able to fuel my motivation, and *then* build that drive and determination I spoke of.

I have no doubt that these things that I'm preaching can help you. Because I have proof that they helped me. This step is about finding more ways to get more of that help. But this is almost the juncture in the process where your journey separates from mine and whoever else might be reading this book. Because there were actual parameters as far as the category in which direction we were deciding to take our growth in, in the previous steps. Spiritually, character, mind, body, learning; this step has none of that. This is where *you* decide what *your* journey will consist more of based on what you know about yourself.

This is also a good place to do a little recap. To get out a sheet of paper and start writing down some of your progress from your journey with these previous steps. What you learned, and what you didn't learn. What you wish you would have learned or gained. Also what you plan to learn moving forward. Jot down some of your wins and your losses. Jot down the pros and cons of each step. This can help you get more of a grasp on exactly where you are now, as opposed to where you began. The more in depth the better. Retrospection is a key component to developing self-awareness, and self-awareness is the key to the ignition to any kind of change anyone seeks to make. This brief side-step of a review of your journey so far, very well could be its very own step. These types of intermissions of reflection are not confined to just this step. It could be and should be continual, and I utilize my journal to accomplish this. Simply reflecting on my day, my week, and/or my month offers me a clean slate and an open space to spend some time with myself; get to know myself better. Even just to clear some thoughts, uncover some future desires, or be grateful for my progress, and the things going well in my life. Journaling for self retrospection has always been one of my first recommended tools I suggest to anyone looking to make strides in self development. It's free, its flexible, and there's no rules to journalling. You just write. So if you already haven't incorporated journaling as part of your routine, now would be a perfect time to give it a try. And with that; you'd be doing more.

This step is simply about compounding our positive steps in the right direction, which will offset all of our negative steps we've took towards the wrong direction in the past; and even the ones we continue to make. Eventually it will start to even out and the more you do, the more you get. And the more steps you take in your new desired direction will bring you closer and closer, until, you inevitably reach your new desired destination. But don't forget to give yourself credit for the steps you've already taken. There's great strength in being grateful for any progress. Results are also a great source of motivation but you have to be aware of your results and your progress to allow them to motivate you.

My first step was reading and learning from a self-help book on how to become more optimistic. I did learn and I did feel more optimistic; that resulted in a better mood which is what prompted me to do more: read the second book. The hope and inspiration that I gained from the Bible, pushed me to learn more about Universal Energy. The core value list practice impacted my character so greatly which prompted me to do more in that area and focus more on other character flaws to improve. The fact that I learned how to be more optimistic proved to me that I could learn anything. So I decided to learn more and took on studying Spanish and studying the electrician handbook for future employment. My workout routine that resulted in 14 lost pounds revealed that I was capable; so I added more workouts, more difficulty, more time, and more diet to see more results.

But this is after I had seen the results. I had proof that putting in the work would reap the benefits. There's only one reason you would do anything mentioned in this book, and that's to see results. I have no doubts that there are some results; whether they are ever-present or the ones you have to take time to uncover. But they are there. Make sure you're aware of how far you've come.

Maybe you're not ready to do more. It's quite possible that you're not at the point where you have been able to notice the results you would have hoped for in the previous steps yet. That's the keyword: YET. There is no reality in which effort, consistency, intention, attention, and energy in any given direction, and in your case, a positive direction, will not bring forth results. You always reap what you sow and we've been planting good seeds so there's no doubt you will reap good fruit in due time. Maybe that time is now and you're ready to plant more good seeds. That's all the step is about; planting more good seeds. It's simple. It falls in no category. There's no parameters, no pressure on how big or little the steps need to be. You're relying on yourself and your own intuition on which way is best for you to continue your progress. That's it.

I love this quote by Arnold Schwarzenegger about why he smiles while he's works out, *"Because I knew that with every rep that I did, with every weight that I lifted, I got one step closer to turning my vision into reality.*" This process is no different. With every page you read, with every day you work on your body, every minute you meditate, every prayer you send up, you're getting closer to realizing that the vision you desire will come to fruition. That's why he smiles. Because he knows that all he has to do is lift the weights and he'll be stronger. Once the strength is gained, and you're stronger, you add more weight. But there is no need to be intimidated because we already gained and earned the strength needed to be capable of lifting these heavier weights. And when you lift *those*, guess what? You get stronger again. There is no other possible outcome. All we have to do is try, and we will see results. When we see results, we'll try a little more. Then we'll see more results.

The big difference between the work we're doing in these steps and weight training is that we're not adding *more* weight. In fact, it'll start to feel like there's a weight being lifted off your shoulders. You'll start feeling lighter, the sun will seem brighter, and that smile he talked about? You'll have it too but it won't be one you'll have to force. It'll start to come naturally, more and more frequently. Just like it did for me when I started realizing that I could try, figure out, analyze, strategize, and learn different ways to grow. When I grew as a result of my own efforts, it was a revelation that I wouldn't change for the world because it was the realization of my capabilities that gave birth to the first sign of belief in myself that I had in years. A belief that I truly lost during my struggles with addiction. When I realized I was capable of changing who I was, and started believing in myself again, it did put a smile on my face. And it did motivate me to do more.

Learning will never stop. Figuring out which way to go and to grow will always evolve, but at this juncture we have a decent idea of what works, what doesn't, and what we'd like to try. In the next step we're going to scrap the learning (as far as instructions for the steps is concerned) and we're going to take a different approach. We're going to get organized. We're going to organize a plan; a plan that will put us on a day-to-day path to overcoming our struggle with addiction. It's going to be a certain plan; a certain plan that we all should have no matter what kind of life we live.

Hardaway Learning Suggestion:

1. Review your progress so far by get a sheet of paper and a pen to write down your progress including the pros and cons of each step so far.

2. Determine which step category was most beneficial to you.

3. Find another exercise within that category, or add more duration to the existing exercise, and supplement it into your day.

Another Option

1. Think of an exercise that hasn't been mentioned or suggested in this book. One outside any of these categories and supplement it into your day. Examples: NA/AA meetings, therapy, volunteer work, a productive hobby, etc.

Chapter 7

Step 7 - Create a Daily Routine

Step seven is to: "Create a daily routine." A daily routine compiled of all the habits, methods, practices and skills that we've learned about throughout the previous chapters in this book about self development. But now we have a good idea of what we like, what we don't, what works, and what won't. Now it's your job to move forward with a daily plan and strategy to ensure that progress can sustain momentum and continue to proceed.

The majority of this book consisted of continuous learning that took place within some of the most common self-development and personal-growth categories out there: spirituality, character, mind, and body. The specificity of that learning did not require any structure, or come with definitive direction outside of the participation within the categorical parameters. That was totally necessary to start the process of self-growth. The beginning of any growth is always to start learning; knowledge gained and wisdom. That was certainly the case for me at the beginning of my journey from addiction to sobriety. At the beginning, I was simply learning, trying new things, and being open minded with the belief that they could help me, and would help me (and they actually did).

As sporadic as the learning might have been for you, with your focus in this direction and that direction, the actual learning itself is the key element to the growth that we hoped to see in the subsequent steps; because learning is the foundation of every form of growth in any form of self development. The best part is that during the process, we relied on ourselves to search in all the different ways to find out which direction and which formula is best for us — what we're capable of doing, what we like to do, what we are willing to do, and what we are willing to keep doing. That's why it's most important for you to keep in mind what's best for you as we move forward to incorporate these things we studied and practiced into a daily routine to develop some positive habits to negate some of the negative habits we've developed over the years; and continue our growth in our new desired positive direction.

Sure, I gave suggestions based on what I've come to understand that helped me most over the years, and what I know about what worked for *me*. But the subsequent steps were about you learning what will work for *you*. It's possible that I forgot to mention many practices, methods and ideas in any one of these previous categories that you already have knowledge about that could help you grow; and that's fine. Implement that. Perhaps your very first "step one" was to read a self-help book that had a completely different chain of steps, or methods, or *ways* that can construct a daily routine that cover most of the categories I mentioned in this book that you really, truly believe could help change your life. That works too.

Similar to a book I read **'Become Unstoppable,'** written by Ben Angel which gave me a step-by-step guide on how to *retool* your life and *rewire* your brain in a 90 day span; the book came with a daily routine and a plan. A lot of which I adopted into my daily routine. Some of it I had already learned previously, so I kept it the same. Some I didn't agree with, so I changed. For example, the part of his mental routine and his version of focusing on the mind is; visualization. I experimented with visualization, but wasn't able to fully grasp the concept in order to see the results I was searching for. His preferred method is visualization. My preferred method is meditation. Very similar daily routines. But I adjusted mine specifically to fit me. And that's what you're expected to do as well when you form your new daily routine.

Flexibility is indispensable for the routine we plan to create in this step. It can be as flexible as it needs to be to fit your life in regards to; time, duration, which areas you focus on most, what time of the day, how long each practice lasts, etc. When I began the process of my growth all the way back to that prison cell from that first step; opening that first self-help book and seeing some results in the growth in my optimism? That was my first step. My results after that? I was motivated to learn more. Learn more I did. And I was all over the place; trying this, doing that, reading this. I was like a kid in a candy store or chicken with its head cut off; but in a good way because I learned a lot. Some of it stuck, some of it didn't. But when I decided to get more serious about my development, and get more disciplined about it, that's when I created a routine to get more structure within my productive habits I developed.

I can still take you through my very first daily routine that I formed (which was also the period in my life when I made the most progress). At any age or stage of my 33-years of living, hands down, it was by far the most substantial period of maturation I've ever experienced. I believe my daily routine was the number one reason why that was the case. The establishment of my daily routine is absolutely the reason my progress moved at an accelerated pace.

First Routine:

6:00 AM: Wake up, Make bed, Pray, Brush teeth

6:10 AM: Read two bible verses

6:30 AM: Journal

7:00 AM: Cell doors unlock, Workout

8:30 AM: Shower, Get dressed

8:45 AM: Read self-help book - Mind is the Master By James Allen, Take notes

10:30 AM: Journal

11:00 AM: Walk around unit, Help people with their treatment work (or) purposely socialize

12:00 PM: Eat first meal of the day (lunch)

12:30 PM: Stretch for outside recreation

1:00 - 3:00 PM: Basketball, Long distance running (or) work out again outside

3:30 PM: Lockdown for count (read self-help book)

4:45 PM: Relax, Eat dinner, Watch TV programs, Leisure time

7:00 PM: Write book (or) learn Spanish

9:00 PM: Read for 30 minutes, Meditate for ten minutes, Pray

9:45 PM: Go to sleep

That's an example of a type of routine we plan to create for ourselves in this step. Now you might notice one big thing: that's an entire full-day routine. I followed that routine for months; it was so effective and it utterly changed my life as it pertains to the drastic mentality shift I gained, the change in the way I thought and conducted myself, which fueled my ability to get, and remain sober. My entire day was filled with productive habits, aimed towards growing a person. When the majority of your time is dedicated to a specific direction, or realizing a particular result: that time, that effort, makes realizing that particular result an absolute certainty. And in my case, and yours, we're searching for growth.

But this type of routine was definitely a beneficiary of being in prison; being the fact that I had no responsibilities or obligations to fulfill, and nothing but time on my hands. But I do give myself credit. Because I did fill that time with productive and constructive positive habits like fitness, learning, and spirituality, which helped me grow as a person daily. Unlike the way some other inmates spent their time. I was absolutely one of those inmates in the past who didn't spend his time wisely. Which was why I was unable to prevent relapse after the numerous prison stints I did before this one. I was *still* one of those inmates well into my 56 month sentence. My day consisted mostly of sitting around, watching TV, playing basketball, gambling, or getting high. Telling myself '*I'm just doing my time*'. I was *doing* my time. But I was going to have to "do the time" regardless, so I might as well utilize my time wisely. And when I made the decision to utilize my time wisely, that's when things finally started to change.

How about how I utilized my time during active addiction? What did my daily routine look like? That's easy. First things first: wake up and get high. That's depending on if I even slept the previous night (or two nights, or three nights). Either case I would start my day off with an 'L'; feeding or continuing my addiction. Next, run the streets of society in attempt to pull off some successful theft, scam, robbery, lie, or some form of crime to secure my next high. After that. I'd get high again. Then I'd go to sleep(or not go to sleep), and repeat the same exact cycle the next day. I followed a routine identical to this for years a time. There is not an exact moment of time, during a routine like this, that is dedicated to, or has any potential for personal growth. And I did not grow. There's no reality where I would.

But when I made that choice, to be selective and productive with how I spent my time, and did less of the things that were keeping me stagnant and unproductive, and replaced them with things that were healthy, constructive, and improvement based; that's when I began to change. Unquestionably, my daily routine was why *this* time, was different from the *last* times.

I'm not expecting anyone to read this and create an entire full day routine of productivity packed action like the one I just mentioned. Especially if you're struggling with an addiction currently. It can be difficult to muster up the energy and motivation to successfully execute all of these tasks. On top of that, some of us just don't have the time for a schedule like this. We have kids, jobs, treatment, doctors appointments, all sorts of obligations that can make it tough. I'm now one of those people. Now that I'm free, my daily routine looks nothing like the one I had in prison. But I still make sure to touch each of my essential self-development category each day. This is my current daily routine:

Current Routine

3:45 AM: Wake Up, Make bed, Pray, Brush teeth, Drink water

4:00 AM: Meditate

4:10 AM: Read Bible, Journal

4:30 AM: Stretch, Yoga, while listening to daily church podcast

5:00 AM: Head to gym (listen to good vibe music for good mood)

5:15 AM: Workout

6:25 AM: Leave gym, Head to work

7:00 AM - 3:30 PM: Work (eat first meal at 11:00 AM)

4:00 PM - 5:30 PM: Relax, Eat dinner, Watch an informal YouTube video, Leisure, Scroll social media, etc.

5:30 PM - 7:00 PM: Write pages in book (or) other necessary obligations

7:00 PM: Phone on DND, No screen time. Read self-help book

7:45 PM: Journal (review day, plan upcoming day)

8:00 PM: Meditate, Pray

8:20 PM: Lights out

This is my daily routine now. The first routine I mentioned I believe is what helped me get sober. My current routine, I believe, is what *keeps* me sober. But it's all part of the same goal and that's to improve and keep progressing. This is how I plan my day to go daily, but of course everything doesn't always go as planned.

It did take a long time for me to get re-acclimated into society, and to be able to manage the anxiety and stress that the real world brings after 48 straight months in prison. It was a struggle initially to give myself the grace and not be so hard on myself when things didn't go as planned: the unexpected happened or a new obligation popped up. For example, job interviews, travel time, community work service, treatment aftercare, distractions, etc. These things have nothing to do with self-development, and coming from prison where my routine was based minute to minute day to day on focusing on my development, I had no interest in them, and despised every obligation that took me away from what I wanted to do(which was work on myself). I did not plan for this initially when I was released because really there is no planning for every detail of real life. At first, I would feel like I was falling behind, not doing enough, and like I was slacking. That's how I made myself feel trying to get into a new routine without the structure and endless time that comes along with serving prison time(which dare I say), in that regard, being in prison was an advantage. But in the real world, where we all live, we don't have that advantage. That's why flexibility and fluidity within the structure of your routine is key. This daily routine is meant to *fit in your life*, not make *your life fit in it*.

Nowadays, I give myself the grace for the unexpected and the unplanned much better than I did in the past. Whether that's a PO visit, random trips to the store, car problems, shoveling snow, therapist appointments, etc. On these days I simply make adjustments to take 30 minutes away from my leisure time. Or if I'm worn out and really want to relax, I only read 30 minutes for that night or cut back on the writing. Whatever adjustment I feel I need to make at that time, I will make. But that's why I utilize those early morning dark hours to my advantage to make sure that I get my essentials in every single day. It's up to you to figure out what your essentials are.

I've never read the book '5 a.m. Club'. But it's a best-selling and trending self-help book. I'm sure you've heard some of the motivational gurus talk about the benefits of waking up early, and I'm positive reasons why I wake up early, align with all the reasons why it's so highly recommended. But why I do it? Is because the prayer, the meditation, the journaling, the Bible, and the working out, have been *essential* to me getting sober and remaining sober. At that time of the upcoming day, there are little distractions, no obligations, and it's just me in a clean slate of time to focus on what I know I need to focus on, to keep progressing, and also start my day off on the right foot. That's a big deal for me; to start my day off with a win and with productivity. I start my day that way and the rest of my day usually follows suit when I'm on point with my morning routine. That's why I believe that the morning routine is the best routine to have. No matter what, every day I do five things that I know will help me grow as a person and that's all we're trying to do at this step: grow on a daily basis.

So enough about me and my routine. What can your routine look like? First, ask yourself some questions. Seriously, get out a piece of paper or a journal and write down questions similar to these and ask yourself questions. Think of the answers thoroughly and write them down. What do you want to do? What do you like to do? What practice was most effective? What category? Spirituality? Physical? Mental? Character? What would you like to make a focal point of your routine? What should you do more of? Do less of? What would you like to try?

There's a very specific reason why making a daily routine is the final step of what I believe can be your seven steps from addiction to sobriety. The key points I've made like building discipline and flexibility, all coincide with that reason. It's about daily progress. Every day, with a daily routine filled with productive, positive, and progressive habits that give us a specific time (or times) throughout the day where our focus is shifted from our destructive actions we are accustomed to, and placed on habits that will help us mature and flourish. This is so that every single day, no matter what we're doing or going through, we're progressive in a different direction than we're used too. And you don't have to wait to get clean to do this or stop using to start a routine. This routine is about progressively changing our mentality and our character, preparing every day regardless of circumstances, for when that opportunity to get clean, presents itself. The opportunity to get clean *will* present itself. Or we'll be preparing ourselves to *make* that opportunity present itself by taking our lives into our own hands; when we feel ready.

Back to my daily routine. It took some time and practice to make the necessary adjustments to be a person that follows a strict routine like the ones I mentioned. Do you think you could make a similar one? The more detail you have, the less confusion you will have, and the more you can focus your energy on the tasks at hand and conserve your mental energy. What are things that there's just *no* getting around? Work, kids, weekly appointments? Can you take all your information that you have in your life, and come up with a specific routine build around those things, and delegate and dedicate your time to participate in things that help you grow daily? A full day routine, is a real concrete plan for growth.

How about not a full day routine. Can you set up a hour in the morning; before you check your messages and social media, to meditate, read the Bible, and do yoga. Then set another hour at night to put your phone on DND, read a self-help book, journal, and pray? What about a different combination of morning/evening routine? Take the first hour of your day to work-out, eat a healthy breakfast, and go about your day. Then at night before you go to sleep you do a meditation practice focusing on the 7 chakras, spend some time learning, and go to sleep at the same time every night to insure you get a healthy 8 hours.

How about right after you get off work you listen to an informal podcast while you eat one healthy meal for dinner. Take some vitamin supplements, start a basic 30-minute workout. All in a two hour span and every day. Maybe you can't fathom carving out a two hour span out of every day. So how about 15 minutes when you wake up to make your bed and pray? 15 minutes at noon, you journal. 30 minutes at 3:00 p.m., you go on a walk. And at 5 o'clock, you send a positive message to a random person on Facebook just to spread some love. Later that night before whatever time you go to sleep you turn your phone off, sit in silence for 15 minutes, and do deep breath work. At the end of the week you go to church every Sunday. That's an easier, more simple daily routine but it doesn't matter how easy or difficult it is. It doesn't have to be hard to do. Every day you are putting the work in and you will see the results from your effort. Results not only in the form of the benefits gained from the particular practice, but also the strengthening of your discipline.

Discipline is one of the most valuable traits you can ever process, but also one of the hardest to build and strengthen. The more discipline you have, the easier it is to strengthen. However, to those who have little discipline to work with initially, it can feel impossible to find a way to establish any discipline to start with to build upon. Especially if you're struggling with an addiction where self-control and discipline are glaring weaknesses; like they were for me when I was addicted. That's where a daily routine comes in handy. Because as long as you come up with your plan, your strategy, your routine, no matter how big or small, or how easy or hard it is, if you stick with it, you're building discipline. This is exactly how I built my first shred of discipline —whereas as an addict— I had zero discipline.

Maybe you're in the middle of your addiction; and it's bad. You have no job, no structure to your life, no sleep schedule, and most of your days consist of coming up with a new plan to score your next high. And you're reading this thinking, '*this guy has no idea what he's talking about.*' But I do because I've been there. I've experienced the lack of motivation, depression, and apathy that comes along with addiction. I understand it. I lived it for years. But is it possible to take one hour a day? Any time, any place, any condition? High, sober, withdrawing, whatever? At noon one day and midnight the next to just say, '*I've got to do this. I need to read this book, journal, and stretch.*' Or for this hour '*I have to meditate, work out, and pray*'. Just for this one hour. For this one day. And that's it. That can be your daily routine. And you simply increase, and work your way up from there. This is you *trying* and that is all you have to do. As minimal as it might sound or feel, these habits compound interest, and they grow overtime. Discipline strengthens and the self-control manifests. The growth in self-control and discipline is what we need to proceed to take bigger, larger, more difficult steps. Add tougher challenges. Make more sacrifices. Add more to our daily routine. But it must start somewhere.

You understand the principle that we can look back and correlate to the negative steps and outcomes in our lives that were caused by our drug addiction, that resulted in the degradation and regression? That very same principle applies to the positive steps and habits that we now seek to incorporate into our future lives, but the outcome is the opposite. It is a succession of progress and ascension. This step, forming a daily routine, is the final step of seven because it is a combination of everything we've learned, compiled into one daily habit that will bring us closer to our goal of achieving sobriety on a daily basis. Every day, we will be moving towards that goal.

I'm sure there is scientific data to backup my theories, and psychology behind some of my suggestions; but I left it out. Also, there are definitely other ways to reach sobriety than my ideas. If you or someone else has a better way, then I'm all for it. Go for it. I promise you, I support all forms of recovery. But among all the theories and concepts, facts, methods, studies and percentages— some of which are nice to know—some of it's not so nice. The one thing you must understand is that you do have to *try* and these seven steps are about you *trying*. Trying with a strategy and a plan so that you can have more confidence with each step you take. If you can't try a lot, try a little. Try every day. Your effort will add up. All your efforts count.

The seventh step is about formulating a plan, relying on our own intuition, figuring out which way is best for us, and for ourselves. It is a strategy to move ourselves gradually closer to sobriety by our own inner strength; by our own human nature and resiliency. The human inner strength is desperately underestimated. We are born with every resource within us that it takes to be capable of overcoming any obstacle placed in front of us but sometimes it has to be built, dug up, and be forced to grow by our own conscious effort. I believe these steps can help you do just that.

You could be reading this book right now thinking, *'this will never work.'* There was a time in my addiction where I'm sure I would have thought the exact same thing, would have not believed, or tried. And I would have stayed the exact same: addicted. Mahatma Gandhi, Muhammad Ali, and Martin Luther King could have did an intervention on me and said *"this book right here is how you do it. This is how you get clean."* And I would have looked at them like they were crazy and walked out. But there's also a reality where I might have paused, gave it a thought, gave it a shot, and tried. That's what I hope you'll do: *try*. That's what I never did. That's why I stayed addicted for so long. Until I finally tried and now I'm not.

I'm no expert. I'm no treatment specialist or drug addiction counselor. But I am an expert drug addict who overcame his demons and has no plans of reverting back to my old ways. I've experienced that lost feeling; the hopelessness, the helplessness, the defeat from all the mistakes and losses over a span of my entire adult life that sapped my faith and my will to live. I've been there. I've been stuck with no motivation, no belief in myself, and every move I made seemed to dig another foot into that 1,000 foot deep hole I'd been digging myself for years. I had no idea which way to go. This is what relates me to you. So while I sat there defeated, addicted, incarcerated, and depressed, every facet of my circumstances and every belief I had of those circumstances convinced me I wasn't capable of overcoming my addiction. I didn't know that that just was not true.

As humans, we're born with everything we need to recover from setbacks. No difficulty can take that from us. No difficulty is unchangeable. As long as you try to change it. You can change it. You have it within you. And if you picked up this book, that means you have a seed planted that you *want* to change or *need* to change. If you read this far, that means you're actively *trying* to change as we speak and that is truly where most people fail; including where I failed in the past. I never *tried*. I don't have all the answers. I don't know every outcome, but nobody does. There is no magic cure for this disease that claims thousands of lives across the globe yearly. No one knows how to fix it. But I do know this for a fact: recovery *is* possible. And it's possible for you, just like it was possible for me.

Hardaway Learning Suggestion:

1. Review everything you've learned about all the practices, methods, and exercises in all previous 6 steps.

2. Pick one practice for each category: Spirituality, Core Value Practice, Mind, Body, Learning

3. Carve out 30 minute time blocks throughout your day for each practice in each category. Preferable at the same time each day. Try your best to account for every hour of your day. Down to the most minute details you can manage to account for.

* For step 6, "Do More.". If the practice chosen in that step falls into a category, make it an hour time block. If it falls outside of any of these categories, add another 30 minutes.

* Preferred time blocks: First thing in the morning or right before bedtime, or both.

Outro

Throughout this book, you may have noticed that I spoke very little on the actual '*action*' of quitting the usage of these drugs, that is the cause the addiction; which is the only way to achieve sobriety. My book focused, mostly more on personal-growth and self-development, and it was intended to be that way. That's because personal-growth and self-development were eminent in my journey from addiction to sobriety. This book is based on what '*I learned*', and what '*I know*', about what '*helped me*' overcome my addiction. But I also '*know*' that there are thousands of people around the world that find themselves and similar shoes as I did: struggling with addictions. Addictions ranging from: alcohol, cocaine, crack, ecstasy, meth, and heroin. Addictions I struggled with in my past. I know these seven steps helped me get, and remain sober. And my hope is they can do the same to help you, or your loved one, or whoever might be struggling with addiction.

But I understand fully that all recovery stories are not linear, and are far from identical. So let me state this clearly: I support all forms of recovery. MAT program, 12 step, NA, AA, inpatient or outpatient treatment. I am a advocate for all forms of recovery, and if you believe you need professional medical attention, or guidance from a licensed counselor or a treatment specialist, I encourage you to seek out that help and pray that you do.

The truth is, that way, might be the best way for you and your journey from addiction to sobriety. If it's treatment, 12 step, MAT, vivitrol, Methadone, complete abstinent like myself, or any of these other forms of recovery that provide you the help you need to live a drug-free, crime free, sober lifestyle (and not my book that does it for you), then I fully support that. I promise you I do. Any way we as a collective society can make drug addiction recovery a more common occurrence, I support.

My book did not come with any scientific backed data, or any 'tried and true' treatment based philosophies because the simple fact that my recovery journey did not take me down that path. That is not to say that I think they aren't effective, or that I would not have been open to treatment or 12 step during my addiction, or believe that they wouldn't have helped me. I do believe they could've help me. That's just not how my sobriety story went.

I have never been a treatment outside of the prison RDAP program, but I would have been open to go the treatment route during my addiction, because I believe it can be effective. I've been to one, seven day detox facility in my life. And that was effective for me get sober for 7 days and proceed with the vivitrol (30 day opiate blocker) treatment. But I was unable to sustain sobriety after the shot wore off, and that's as far as the professional help went for me.

My sobriety journey, now at about three years of complete abstinence, took me a different route. About a 14 year span from ages 18-31, where I spent every day as an alcoholic, a drug addict or an inmate, only able to maintain any significant length of sobriety during my periods of my many incarcerations. Until my last prison stint; a 56 month federal prison sentence where I actually was able to maintain a drug addiction that carried on from the streets about two years into my sentence.

And that's where my story started to turn for the better. That's where I learned to change. That's where my story changed. From an addiction story, to a sobriety story. That's what inspired me to write this book. I'm not expecting anybody to read these seven steps, and instantly snap into sobriety. Recovery is a journey. A process. But I am 100% confident that these steps can help you progress along that process.

I don't have all the answers. I don't have all the outcomes. But you know what? No one does. But I do think we need more perspectives, more voices, more hope, more inspiration, more first hand information —to give the addiction community— more life. And if my book can do any one of those things, for any one person, that's all I could hope for.

Thank You for reading.

Sincerely,

Derrick Moore

References

(1) Bishop, G. (2017). Unf*ck yourself: get out of your head and into your life. London,   UK. Yellow Kite.

(2) Davenport, B. & Scott, S.J. (2016). Declutter your mind: how to stop worrying.   relieve anxiety. and eliminate negative thinking. Oldtown Publishing.

Connect with Hardaway Learning across Social Media

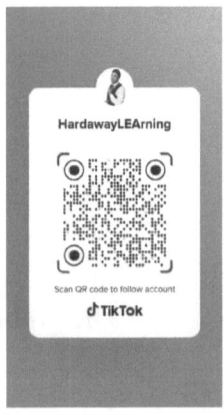

Made in United States
Troutdale, OR
11/01/2024

24345432R00094